Michael Price

Excel
2010

In easy steps is an imprint of In Easy Steps Limited
Southfield Road · Southam
Warwickshire CV47 0FB · United Kingdom
www.ineasysteps.com

Notice of Liability
Every effort has been made to ensure that this book contains accurate
and current information. However, In Easy Steps Limited and the
author shall not be liable for any loss or damage suffered by readers
as a result of any information contained herein.

Trademarks
Microsoft® and Windows® are registered trademarks of Microsoft
Corporation. All other trademarks are acknowledged as belonging to
their respective companies.

In Easy Steps Limited supports The Forest Stewardship Council (FSC),
the leading international forest certification organisation. All our titles
that are printed on Greenpeace approved FSC certified paper carry the
FSC logo.

MIX
Paper from
responsible sources
FSC® C020837

Printed and bound in the United Kingdom

ISBN 978-1-84078-404-6

Contents

1 Introduction

This chapter shows how the spreadsheet, the electronic counterpart of the paper ledger, has evolved in Excel, taking advantage of the features of the associated versions of Microsoft Office, and the operating systems (Windows 7, Windows Vista, and Windows XP).

The Spreadsheet Concept

Spreadsheets, in the guise of the accountant's ledger sheet, have been in use for many, many years. They consisted of paper forms with a two-dimensional grid of rows and columns, often on extra-large paper, forming two pages of a ledger book for example (hence the term spreadsheet). They were typically used by accountants to prepare budget or financial statements. Each row would represent a different item, with each column showing the value or amount for that item over a given time period. For example, a forecast for a 30% margin and 10% growth might show:

Margin %	30				
Growth %	10				
			Profit Forecast		
	January	February	March	April	May
Cost of Goods	6,000	6,600	7,260	7,986	8,785
Sales	7,800	8,580	9,438	10,382	11,420
Profit	1,800	1,980	2,178	2,396	2,635
Total Profit	1,800	3,780	5,958	8,354	10,989

Any changes to the basic figures would mean that all the values would have to be recalculated and transcribed to another ledger sheet to show the effect, e.g. for a 20% margin and 60% growth:

Margin %	20				
Growth %	60				
			Profit Forecast		
	January	February	March	April	May
Cost of Goods	6,000	9,600	15,360	24,576	39,322
Sales	7,200	11,520	18,432	29,491	47,186
Profit	1,200	1,920	3,072	4,915	7,864
Total Profit	1,200	3,120	6,192	11,107	18,972

To make another change, to show 10% margin and 200% growth, for example, would involve a completely new set of calculations. And, each time, there would be the possibility of a calculation or transcription error creeping in.

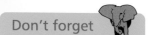
With the advent of the personal computer, a new approach became possible. Applications were developed to simulate the operation of the financial ledger sheet, but the boxes (known as cells) that formed the rows and columns could store text, numbers, or a calculation formula based on the contents of other cells. The spreadsheet looked the same, since it was the results that were displayed, rather than the formulas themselves. However, when the contents of a cell were changed in the spreadsheet, all the cells whose values depended on that changed cell were automatically recalculated.

...ovement in productivity
...g. In the example shown
...et using formulas, rather
...es. Your spreadsheet might
...r example:

...cells are the actual values
...e contents of other cells:

	Forecast	
ch	April	May
7260	7986	8785
9438	10382	11420
2178	2396	2635
5958	8354	10989

...nges, different values for
...hange just those items and
...culated by the formulas are

...ications have evolved, and
...beyond the original use
...ey can now handle any
...terrelated by formulas,
...experimental data, or
...for example. In fact, the
...support just about any

Microsoft Excel

VisiCalc and Lotus 123 were MS-DOS programs, subject to its command-line interface, but Microsoft Excel was developed for Windows. It was the first spreadsheet program to allow users to control the visual aspects of the spreadsheet (fonts, character attributes, and cell appearance). It introduced intelligent cell recomputation, where only cells dependent on the cell being modified are updated (previous spreadsheet programs recomputed everything all the time, or waited for a specific Recalc command).

Later versions of Excel were shipped as part of the bundled Microsoft Office suite of applications, which included programs like Microsoft Word and Microsoft PowerPoint.

Versions of Excel for Microsoft Windows and Office include:

1987	Excel 2.0	Windows
1990	Excel 3.0	Windows
1992	Excel 4.0	Windows
1993	Excel 5.0	Windows
1995	Excel 95 (v7.0)	Office 95
1997	Excel 97 (v8.0)	Office 97
1999	Excel 2000 (v9.0)	Office 2000
2001	Excel 2002 (v10)	Office XP
2003	Excel 2003 (v11)	Office 2003
2007	Excel 2007 (v12)	Office 2007
2010	Excel 2010 (v14)	Office 2010

The newer versions of Excel provide many enhancements to the user interface, and incorporate connections with Microsoft Office and other applications. The basis of the program, however, remains the same. It still consists of a large array of cells, organized into rows and columns, and containing data values or formulas with relative or absolute references to other cells. This means that many of the techniques and recommendations included in this book will be applicable to whichever version of Excel you may be using, or even if you are using a spreadsheet from another family of products, though, of course, the specifics of the instructions may need to be adjusted.

Don't forget

Microsoft Multiplan, the predecessor of Excel, was an MS-DOS program. There were also Apple Mac versions of Excel, starting with Excel 1.0.

10

Don't forget

Originally, the program was referred to by the full name, Microsoft Excel, since the name Excel belonged to a financial software program. However, Microsoft now owns that trademark, so this distinction is no longer necessary.

Microsoft Office 2010

Microsoft Office 2010 is the latest version of Microsoft Office, and it is available in a variety of editions, including:

- Office 2010 Home and Student
- Office 2010 Home and Business
- Office 2010 Standard
- Office 2010 Professional
- Office 2010 Professional Academic
- Office 2010 Professional Plus

All these editions include Microsoft Excel, and the application is also available as a separate, stand-alone product. In either case, Excel 2010 incorporates the Office result-oriented user interface, with the Ribbon, File tab, BackStage, Galleries, and Live Preview, etc.

Excel 2010 also uses the Microsoft Office file format, OpenXML, as the default file format. This is based on XML and uses ZIP compression, so the files will be up to 75% smaller than those in the older Microsoft Office file formats.

Other shared Office features include the Document Theme, which defines colors, fonts, and graphic effects for a spreadsheet or other Office document, and collaboration services for sharing spreadsheets and documents with other users.

- Office 2010 Starter Edition

Some computers may be supplied with a limited Office 2010 edition, which includes starter editions of Word and Excel. These exclude functions, such as macros, add-ins, full screen view, customizable ribbon, and quick access toolbar.

- Office Web Apps

Microsoft offers a free, web-based version of Office, this includes online versions of Word, Excel, PowerPoint, and OneNote. These web apps feature user interfaces similar to the full desktop products, and allow you to share documents with users who may not have Office 2010 on their systems.

Hot tip

You may sometimes see this product referred to as Office 14, this is the internal numbering system used by the Microsoft development teams.

Don't forget

The Office Starter edition replaces the Microsoft Works office product, which is no longer being marketed.

Features of Excel 2010

Don't forget

A spreadsheet in Excel contains multiple sheets, each of which is known as a Worksheet. The set of worksheets in an Excel file forms a Workbook.

In addition to the features Microsoft Office 2010 shares with the other Office applications, Microsoft Excel has its own, exclusive features. These include:

1 Worksheets can have up to 1,048,576 rows and 16,384 columns, rather than the previous limits of 65,536 by 256

2 Color Scales, Icon Sets, and Data Bars apply conditional formatting, based on the values of cells in a group

3 Page Layout view allows you to create and update spreadsheets as they will appear when printed

4 The charting engine includes 3D rendering, transparencies and shadows, and will highlight trends in the data

 5 Sparklines - tiny charts that fit in a single cell - help to visually summarize trends in your data (see page 178)

System Requirements

To install and run Excel 2010, your computer should match or better the minimum hardware and operating system requirements for Office 2010. If you are upgrading to Office 2010, from Office 2007, the hardware should already meet the requirements, though you may need to upgrade your operating system. For an upgrade from Office 2003, you will need to check that both hardware and operating system meet the minimum specifications for Office 2010, this includes:

Operating system	Windows XP SP3 (32-bit), Windows Vista SP2 or Windows 7 (32 or 64-bit)
Processor speed	500 MHz or higher
Memory	256 MB or higher
Devices	DVD drive
Hard disk	3.52 GB available space for installation
Monitor	1024x768 resolution or higher
Internet connection	Broadband connection recommended for download and product activation

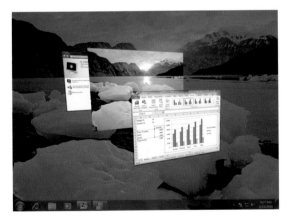

Additional Software Requirements
If you have another computer still running an older version of Office, and you need to work with Excel files that are in the Office 2010 format, you might download the Microsoft Office Compatibility Pack, from www.microsoft.com/downloads. This will allow older versions of Excel to read the new file format.

The Office 2010 Ribbon

The menus and toolbars that were used in previous versions of Excel used a top-down approach, which made it difficult to find the appropriate tools. These have now been replaced by the Ribbon. With this, commands are organized in logical groups, under command tabs. These include the Home, Insert, Page Layout, Formulas, Data, and Review tabs, and they follow the order in which tasks are normally performed. When you click any of these tabs, the corresponding commands are displayed in the Ribbon.

The Ribbon may also include contextual command tabs, which appear when you perform a specific task. For example, if you select some data and then click the Column button in Charts, the chart tool tabs, Design, Layout, and Format, will be displayed.

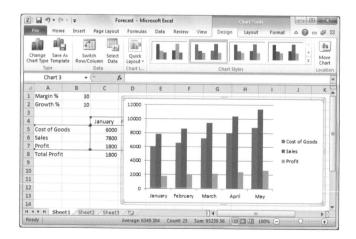

You can minimize the Ribbon, to make more room available on the screen. You'll still be able to access the commands on the Ribbon by redisplaying the Ribbon as a temporary overlay, or by using shortcut keys (see page 118).

Office Starter Edition

If your computer has Office Starter edition preinstalled, you must select the version of Office to install before you can run Excel.

1 Select Start, and then click Microsoft Office 2010

Don't forget

You can choose to activate an existing license for Office 2010, go online to purchase a copy, or use Office Starter 2010.

2 To install Office Starter 2010, click the Use button

3 The Office Starter 2010 contents are listed, and you are given another opportunity to purchase Office. Click the Open button to confirm you want Office Starter

Excel Starter 2010

  Select Start, All Programs, Microsoft Office Starter, and then choose Microsoft Excel Starter 2010

2 Excel Starter 2010 opens, ready for you to create and edit spreadsheets, as with any version of Excel

Excel Starter uses the Ribbon interface, but it has fewer functions than the full Excel 2010, as shown by the reduced number of tabs

Excel 2010 and Windows XP

If you have Office 2010 on your system (or if you purchase it from Office Starter), you can start the full Excel 2010.

When your system is running under Windows XP:

1 Click the Start button, click All Programs, and then click Microsoft Office

2 Click Microsoft Excel 2010

This starts up the full version of Excel 2010, with the same interface and functions that you find in Excel 2010 running under Windows Vista or Windows 7 (as used for the examples and illustrations in this book).

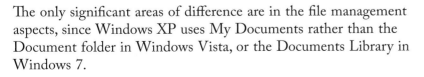

The only significant areas of difference are in the file management aspects, since Windows XP uses My Documents rather than the Document folder in Windows Vista, or the Documents Library in Windows 7.

The Excel functions and procedures are the same, whichever operating system you are using.

Windows XP does not offer the Start Menu Search box provided in Windows Vista and Windows 7 (see page 18), so you must navigate through the Start menu.

Right-click the Excel 2010 entry and select Pin to Start menu, you'll now be able to select Excel 2010 from the top of the Start menu in future.

Excel 2010 and Windows 7

Don't forget

Under Windows Vista or Windows 7, you can select Start, type the program name Excel, and select the program entry, listed at the top of the Start menu.

With Excel installed under Windows 7, you will use the new style Start menu to begin running Excel 2010.

1 Click the Start button and move the mouse pointer over the All Programs entry

2 When the program list appears, click Microsoft Office, and select Microsoft Office Excel 2010

3 Excel 2010 starts ready for you to create or edit spreadsheets

Hot tip

The Excel window will exhibit transparency effects, if your Windows 7 (or Windows Vista) system is Aero-enabled.

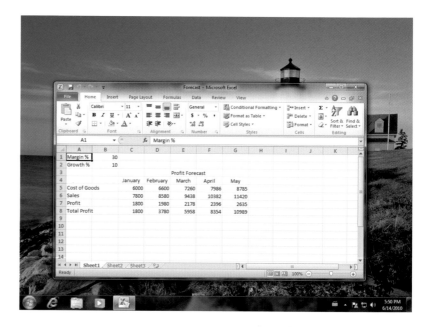

4 Right-click the icon on the taskbar and select Pin this program to taskbar, to provide a quick launch for Excel, under Windows 7

Menu to Ribbon Reference

 1 At office.microsoft.com, click Get help finding commands

 2 Select the link for Office 2010 Interactive Guides

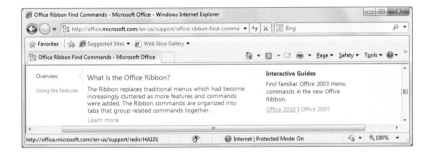

19

 3 Scroll down to Get a printable list, and select Get the Office 2010 menu-to-ribbon reference workbooks

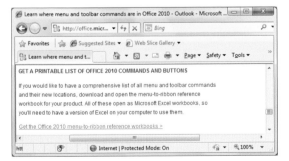

4 Select the Excel Menu to ribbon, and click the Download button to transfer the file to your computer

...cont'd

5 Save the template to your hard drive

6 The template will open in an Excel window

There is a worksheet for each of the menu and toolbar names from Excel 2003. For example, the Insert Menu worksheet lists the commands now located on various Excel 2010 tabs.

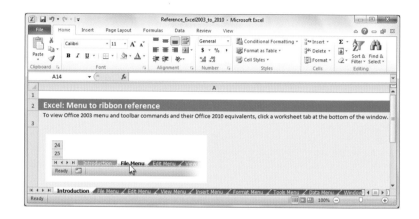

Hot tip

To search for a specific command, click the Home tab, and then click Find & Select, and Find, then type in the command name you wish to locate.

20

2 Begin with Excel

We start with a simple workbook, to show what's involved in entering, modifying, and formatting data, and in performing calculations. This includes ways in which Excel helps to minimize the effort. We cover printing, look at Excel Help, and discuss the various file formats associated with Excel.

The Excel Window

Don't forget

Workbook is the term Microsoft uses for a set of Excel spreadsheets.

When you start Excel, it displays the Excel window with a blank workbook called Book1.

Quick Access Toolbar

Command tabs

Title bar with file name

Minimize or Expand Ribbon

Help

File tab

Office Ribbon with commands

Group

Name box

Formula bar

Worksheet

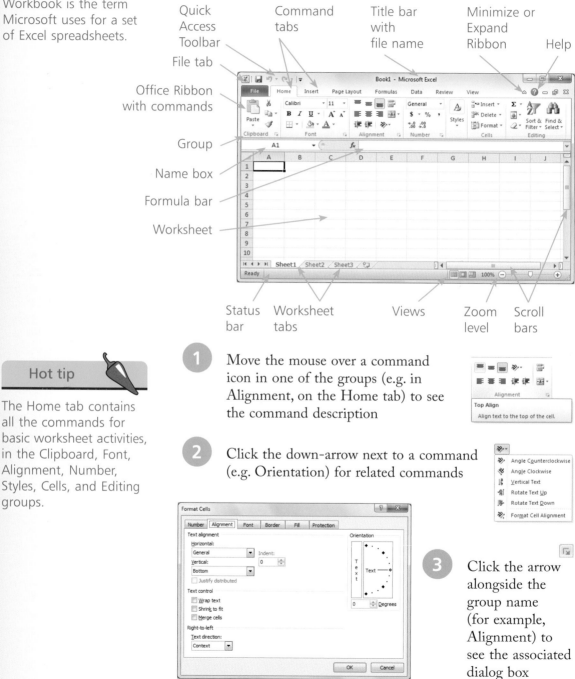

Status bar

Worksheet tabs

Views

Zoom level

Scroll bars

Hot tip

The Home tab contains all the commands for basic worksheet activities, in the Clipboard, Font, Alignment, Number, Styles, Cells, and Editing groups.

1 Move the mouse over a command icon in one of the groups (e.g. in Alignment, on the Home tab) to see the command description

2 Click the down-arrow next to a command (e.g. Orientation) for related commands

3 Click the arrow alongside the group name (for example, Alignment) to see the associated dialog box

By default, Excel provides three separate arrays of data (known as worksheets) in the workbook. These are named Sheet1, Sheet2, and Sheet3. Each worksheet is the equivalent of a full spreadsheet and has the potential for up to 1,048,576 x 16,384 cells, arranged in rows and columns.

The rows are numbered 1, 2, 3 and onwards, up to a maximum of 1,048,576. The columns are lettered A to Z, AA to ZZ, and then AAA to XFD. This gives a maximum of 16,384 columns. The combination gives a unique reference for each cell, from A1 right up to XFD1048576.

Hot tip

One worksheet is usually all you need to create a spreadsheet, but it can sometimes be convenient to organize the data into several worksheets.

Only a very few of these cells will be visible at any one time, but any part of the worksheet can be displayed on the screen, which acts as a rectangular porthole onto the whole worksheet.

⌐A1

ZZ255⌐

Use the scroll bars to reposition the screen view, or type a cell reference into the name box, e.g. ZZ255.

See page 44 for other ways to navigate through the worksheet, using the arrow keys, scroll functions, and split views.

XFD1048576⌐

Beware

These are the theoretical limits for worksheets. For very large numbers of records, a database program may be a more suitable choice.

23

Don't forget

The actual number of cells shown depends on your screen resolution, the cell size, and the mode of display (e.g. with the Ribbon minimized, or in full screen view).

Create a Workbook

We will start by creating a simple, personal budget workbook, to illustrate the processes involved in creating and updating your Excel spreadsheet.

1 When Excel opens, it displays the blank workbook Book1, which can be used as the starting point for your new workbook

2 If you want a fresh, empty spreadsheet, click the File tab and select New. Double-click the Blank workbook (or select the template and press the Create button)

3 A new workbook will be opened, called Book2 (or whatever is the next sequential number)

4 Type the spreadsheet title My Personal Budget in cell A1, and press the down-arrow, or the Enter key, to go to cell A2 (or just click cell A2 to select it)

Add Data to the Worksheet

1 Continue to add text to the cells in column A, pressing the down-arrow or Enter to move down after each, to create labels in cells A2 to A13:

Income
Salary
Interest/dividend
Total income
Expenses
Mortgage/rent
Utilities
Groceries
Transport
Insurance
Total expenses
Savings/shortage

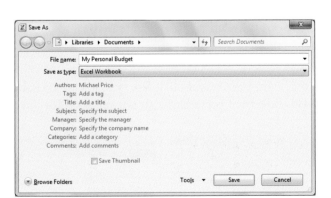

Hot tip

If the text is already available in another document, you can copy and paste the information, to save typing.

2 Click the File tab, and select Save (or press the Ctrl+S keyboard shortcut)

3 Type a file name, e.g. My Personal Budget, and click Save, to add the workbook to the Documents library

Beware

Save the workbook regularly while creating or updating spreadsheets, or you run the risk of losing the work you've done, if a problem arises with the system.

Note that you can add information to classify the document, such as Tag words, Title, or Subject. If you create numerous documents, these details can help you manage and locate your documents and workbooks.

Build the Worksheet

We want to fill in the columns of data for each month of the year, but first, we need an extra row after the title, for the column headings. To add a row to the worksheet:

1 Select the row (click the row number) above where you want to insert another row, e.g. select row 2

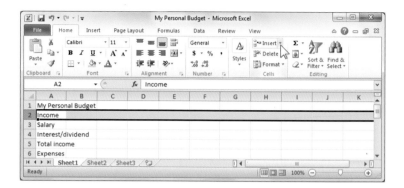

2 Click the Home tab and then, in the Cells group, click the arrow next to Insert, and click Insert Sheet Rows

3 Click cell B2 in the new row, and type January, then press Enter twice, to move to B4

4 Type 3950 in cell B4, press Enter, type 775 in cell B5, and press Enter again

5 In cell B6 type = and click B4, type + and click B5 (to get =B4+B5), then press Enter to see the total displayed in B6

6 Click cell B8, and then type the values 2250, 425, 1150, 350, and 450 (pressing the down-arrow or Enter after each)

7 In cell B13, type =SUM(and then click B8, type a period, click B12, type) and press Enter, then click B13 to see the Formula bar contents

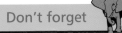

Don't forget

You can click B13 and then click the AutoSum button in the Editing group on the Home tab. This automatically sums the adjacent cells, in this case the five cells above, giving =SUM(B8:B12). See page 68 for more details of AutoSum.

Some of the labels in column A appear truncated. The full label is still recorded, but the part that overlapped column B cannot be displayed, if the adjacent cell is occupied.

To change the column width to fit the contents

1 Select the column of labels (click the letter heading)

2 On the Home tab, in the Cells group, select Format

3 Under Cell Size, select AutoFit Column Width

Don't forget

Column width is measured in characters (assuming a standard font). The default is 8.43, but you can set any value from 0 to 255.

27

Hot tip

To change a group of columns, select the first, hold down Shift and select the last. For non-adjacent columns, select the first, hold down Ctrl and click other columns.

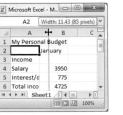

4 Alternatively, move the mouse pointer over the column boundary, and drag to manually widen or double-click to Autofit to contents

Fill Cells

We've typed January, but the rest of the monthly headings can be automatically completed, using the Fill handle.

1 Select B2, the cell with the January heading

2 Move the mouse over the Fill handle

3 Click and drag to adjacent cells

4 Release the mouse button when you have sufficient cells

5 Change the fill options, when necessary, to copy cell contents or to fill with or without formatting

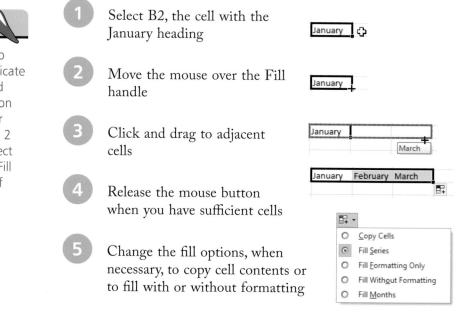

Excel understands a variety of entry types. If you start with Jan, rather than January, you'll fill adjacent cells with Feb, Mar, Apr, etc.

1 Select cell B4, and fill cells C4:G4 with a copy of B4. Repeat for B6 to C6:G6, and for B13 to C13:G13. Select the block of cells B8:B9, and fill cells C8:G9

Complete the Worksheet

1 Select cell H2, and type Period as the heading

2 Select cells B4 to G4, click AutoSum in Editing, on the Home tab, and the total is entered in cell H4

3 Select cell H4, and fill cells H5 to H14, then select cell H7 and press Delete (no total is needed for this row)

4 Select cell B14, type =B6-B13, then press Enter (type the whole formula, or select the cells to add their addresses)

5 Select cell B14, then drag and fill to copy the formula, for Total Income - Total Expenses, to the cells C14:G14

Don't forget

It is sometimes more efficient to fill a whole range of cells, then clear the ones that are not necessary.

29

Hot tip

Since only one worksheet is needed, you can right-click the tabs in turn to Delete Sheet2 and Sheet3, and Rename Sheet1, to My Personal Budget for example.

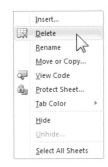

Format the Text

Although not essential for the actual functioning, formatting the text can make it easier to handle the workbook, and make prints more readable.

There are numerous changes that you could make, but, at this stage, we will just make some changes to font size and styles, and to the text placement.

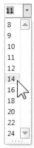

1 Click cell A3, press Ctrl, and click cells A6, A7, A13 and A14, then click the arrow next to Font Size (in the Home tab Font group) and select size 14, click the Bold font button

2 Click column label cell B2, press Shift and click cell H2, and then select font size 14, Bold for cells B2:H2, and select Align Text Right in the Home, Alignment group

3 Select cell range A1 to H1, then, on the Home tab, select Merge and Center in the Home, Alignment group, and select font size 20, Bold for the workbook title

	A	B	C	D	E	F	G	H
1		**My Personal Budget**						
2		Jan	Feb	Mar	Apr	May	Jun	Period
3	**Income**							
4	Salary	3950	3950	3950	3950	3950	3950	23700
5	Interest/dividend	775						775
6	**Total income**	4725	3950	3950	3950	3950	3950	24475
7	**Expenses**							
8	Mortgage/rent	2250	2250	2250	2250	2250	2250	13500
9	Utilities	425	425	425	425	425	425	2550
10	Groceries	1150						1150
11	Transport	350						350
12	Insurance	450						450
13	**Total expenses**	4625	2675	2675	2675	2675	2675	18000
14	**Savings/shortage**	100	1275	1275	1275	1275	1275	6475

4 Click the Save button on the Quick Access toolbar

Number Formats

To apply a specific format to numbers in your worksheet:

1 Select the cells that you wish to reformat, and click the down-arrow in the Number Format box

3950	3950	3950	3950	3950	3950	23700
775	567.75					1342.75
4725	4517.75	3950	3950	3950	3950	25042.75
2250	2250	2250	2250	2250	2250	13500
425	425.04	425	425	425	425	2550.04
1150	1124.9					2274.9
350	437.5					787.5
450	450					900
4625	4687.44	2675	2675	2675	2675	20012.44
100	-169.69	1275	1275	1275	1275	5030.31

General
$ ▾ %
.0 .00
.00 →.0
Number

More Number Formats...

2 Select More Number Formats, and then choose, for example, Number, 2 decimal places, and Red for negative numbers

Format Cells

Number | Alignment | Font | Border | Fill | Protection

Category:
General
Number
Currency
Accounting
Date
Time
Percentage
Fraction
Scientific
Text
Special
Custom

Sample
3950.00

Decimal places: 2

☐ Use 1000 Separator (,)

Negative numbers:
-1234.10
1234.10
(1234.10)
(1234.10)

Number is used for general display of numbers. Currency and Accounting offer specialized formatting for monetary value.

OK | Cancel

3 Click OK, to apply the format to the selection

4 Change the column widths, if required, to display the full numbers (see page 27)

Don't forget

The General format isn't consistent. Decimal places vary, and Excel may apply rounding, to fit numbers in if the column is too narrow.

3950	3950	3950
568	567.75	567.75
4518	4517.8	4517.75
2250	2250	2250
425	425.04	425.04
1125	1124.9	1124.9
438	437.5	437.5
450	450	450
4687	4687.4	4687.44
-170	-169.7	-169.69

31

Hot tip

See page 58 for details on the various types of formats available for numbers in cells.

My Personal Budget - Microsoft Ex...

File | Home | Insert | Page L | Formu | Data | Reviev | View

A16

	A	B	C	D	E
1	**My Personal Budget**				
2		Jan	Feb	Mar	Apr
3	**Income**				
4	Salary	3950.00	3950.00	3950.00	3950.00
5	Interest/dividend	775.00	567.75		
6	**Total income**	4725.00	4517.75	3950.00	3950.00
7	**Expenses**				
8	Mortgage/rent	2250.00	2250.00	2250.00	2250.00
9	Utilities	425.00	425.04	425.00	425.00
10	Groceries	1150.00	1124.90		
11	Transport	350.00	437.50		
12	Insurance	450.00	450.00		
13	**Total expenses**	4625.00	4687.44	2675.00	2675.00
14	**Savings/shortage**	100.00	169.69	1275.00	1275.00

My Personal Budget

Ready | 100%

Print the Worksheet

1 Select the worksheet you want to print (if there's more than one) and click the File tab then Print

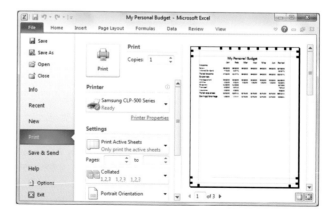

2 You'll see the print options, plus the print preview for your current worksheet

3 Check to see exactly what data will be printed, especially if there are more pages than you were expecting

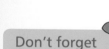
Excel will select a print area that includes all cells that appear to have data in them (including blanks). If you ever scroll past the end of the data, and accidently click a key or the spacebar, Excel will think this is part of the worksheet data and may select a larger print area than you might have anticipated.

4 Click the Printer button to change the printer, if desired

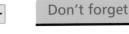
Samsung CLP-500 Series
Ready

5 Click the Print setting, to choose between the active sheet, the entire workbook, and the current selection

Print Active Sheets
Only print the active sheets

Print Active Sheets
Only print the active sheets

Print Entire Workbook
Print the entire workbook

Print Selection
Only print the current selection

Ignore Print Area

6 Other Print Settings allows you to choose the pages to print and to specify duplex, orientation, and paper size

7 Specify the number of copies, then click the Print button to send the document to the printer

Print
Copies: 1

Print

If there is a print area defined, Excel will only print that part of the worksheet. If you don't want to limit the print this time, select "Ignore print areas".

For printing part of the worksheet, you can preset the print area:

1 Select the range of cells that you normally want printed

33

Hot tip

If you are sure that the default print settings are what you require, you can add the Quick Print button to the Quick Access toolbar (see page 119) and use this to start the print immediately.

2 Select the Page Layout tab, click the Print Area button, in the Page Setup group, and select Set Print Area

Print Area
Set Print Area
Clear Print Area

Insert, Copy and Paste

You can rearrange the contents of the worksheet, or add new data, by inserting rows or columns and copying cells. For example, to add an additional 6 months of information:

 Click in column H, press Shift, and click in column M

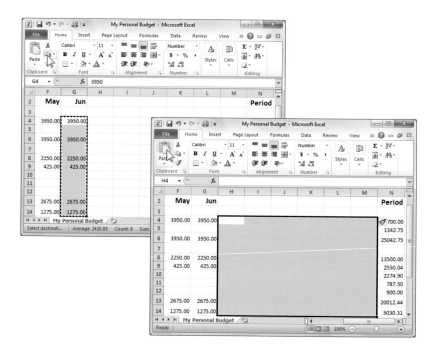

 Select the Home tab, then, in the Cells group, click the arrow next to Insert and choose Insert Sheet Columns

 Select the range G4:G14, click the Copy button 📋 , select the range H4:M14, and click the Paste button 📋

Excel Help

There are several ways to display the Help facility for Excel:

1 Click the question-mark icon on the right of the Excel window

2 Select the File tab, click Help, then choose Microsoft Office Help

3 Press the F1 key

Each of these methods displays the main browser-style Help window, at the Home page, with the top-level list of contents, with getting started and browsing options.

For more specific help:

1 Type keywords into the search box, and press the Search button to list related articles, in blocks of 25 at a time

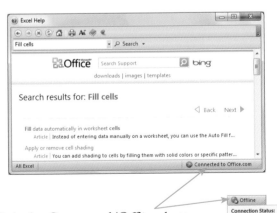

2 Click the Connected/Offline button, to choose content from the computer or from the Office Online website

Contextual Help

You do not always need to search for help – you can get specific information on a particular command or operation.

1 Open a command tab, then move the mouse pointer over a command in one of the groups to reveal the tooltip

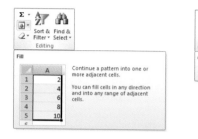

2 If you see the Help icon at the foot of the tooltip, press F1 (with the tooltip still visible) to see the relevant article

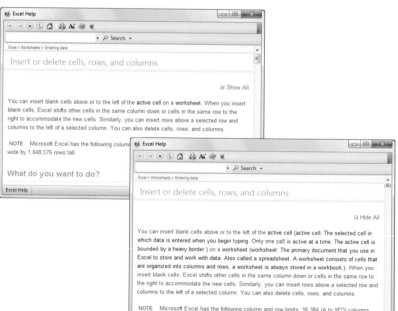

3 Click Show All, to expand the text and include the definitions for particular terms within the article

36

Excel File Formats

When you save a workbook in Excel 2010 (see page 25), it uses the default file type .xlsx. To save your workbook in the format used by previous versions of Excel:

 Click the File tab and select Save As

 Click the box Save as type, and select Excel 97–2003 Workbook

(see page 25)

Save As

File name: My Personal Budget

Save as type: Excel Workbook

Excel Workbook
Excel Macro-Enabled Workbook
Excel Binary Workbook
Excel 97-2003 Workbook
XML Data
Single File Web Page
Web Page
Excel Template
Excel Macro-Enabled Template
Excel 97-2003 Template
Text (Tab delimited)
Unicode Text
XML Spreadsheet 2003
Microsoft Excel 5.0/95 Workbook
CSV (Comma delimited)
Formatted Text (Space delimited)
Text (Macintosh)
Text (MS-DOS)
CSV (Macintosh)
CSV (MS-DOS)
DIF (Data Interchange Format)
SYLK (Symbolic Link)
Excel Add-In
Excel 97-2003 Add-In
PDF
XPS Document
OpenDocument Spreadsheet

 Change the file name, if desired, and click the Save button

Save As

File name: My Personal Budget

Save as type: Excel 97-2003 Workbook

Authors: Michael Price   Tags: Add a tag
☐ Save Thumbnail

Browse Folders   Tools ▼   Save   Cancel

 If you retained the original file name, you will find two files of the same name, but of different types, in your Documents library

You can save your workbooks in a variety of other file formats, which will make it easier to share information with others, who may not have the same applications software.

Hot tip

You can also display the Save As dialog by pressing the F12 key.

1 Click the File tab, select Save As and choose the format you want to use, for example, CSV (Comma deliminated)

2 You may be warned of potential conflicts. For example, you should use negative signs or brackets in numbers rather than the red code, since colors are removed

Don't forget

Text (Tab delimited) or CSV (Comma delimited) formats are often used to exchange information, since most applications will support these.

3 Text and number formatting will be removed, and only the current worksheet is saved.

If there's more than one worksheet in your workbook, you'll need to save each one to a separate file.

3 Manage Data

This chapter introduces navigation tools, commands, and facilities, to enable you to find your way around and work with large spreadsheets. It shows how existing data can be imported into Excel, to avoid having to retype information.

Use Existing Data

If the information you want to add to a workbook already exists in another application, you may be able to import it into Excel and use it without having to retype the data, as long as you can prepare it in a suitable file format.

To identify the file types that can be opened directly in Excel:

1 Select the Office button, and click Open (or press Ctrl+O)

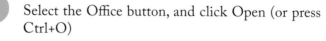

Hot tip

If you clear the box "Hide extensions for known file types" in the Windows Folder Options, you'll see the full details for the supported file types.

2 Click the file type box, alongside the file name box

3 Identify a file type supported by the other application (e.g. Text or CSV) and then click Cancel

4 Extract data from the other application, as that file type

For example, you might have a large number of MP3 tracks created by transferring your CD collection to the hard drive.

Don't forget

Details of the music are downloaded from the Internet when you transfer the tracks to the hard disk, using an application like Windows Media Player. It also records the settings used for the conversion to MP3.

Each file stores particulars of the music it contains, including title, album, artist, composer, recording date, quality (the bit rate used for conversion), genre, etc. These are held in the form of MP3 tags, and an application, such as MP3 Tag Tools, can scan the files and extract the tags, allowing you to make changes or corrections.

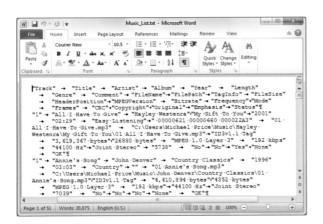

Don't forget

This is just an illustration of how you might extract data from an existing application. Whatever the contents, most applications provide a method for exporting data, usually to a text file format.

You can scan all the music files at once, and then Export the tags. This will generate a tab-delimited text file, with data fields enclosed in quotation marks and paragraph marks between the individual lines.

Hot tip

Empty data items (null values) are represented by a pair of adjacent quotation marks, set between two tab marks. Track lengths are shown as times (mm:ss).

The first line gives field names for data items, and each subsequent line relates to one MP3 file (usually one track of an album), with values for all data items in the same sequence as the field names.

Import Data

1 Select Open from the File tab, change the file type to Text, select the data file you exported, and click Open

Hot tip

Select the file type you used to export data from the application, and follow the prompts. This example shows the process for text files.

2 This launches the Text Import Wizard, which assesses your file and chooses the appropriate settings

Don't forget

Check the settings applied by the import wizard, and make any changes that are required for your particular files.

3 Adjust the delimiters and the text qualifier for your file, if any changes are needed, and preview the effect

4 Review each column, decide whether you want to skip that data item, change the format, or accept the suggestion

Don't forget

The General data format is the most flexible, it interprets numerical values as dates, leaving all other values as text.

5 Click the Finish button to load the data into your Excel worksheet, with lines as rows and data items as columns

43

6 Select Save As, from the File tab, change the file type to Excel Workbook and press the Save button

Beware

The worksheet will be saved as a text file, and will overwrite your original import file unless you save the worksheet as an Excel Workbook, or as another file type.

Navigate the Worksheet

If you've transferred information from an existing application and then find yourself with some rather large worksheets, you'll welcome the variety of ways Excel provides to move around the worksheet.

Arrow keys

 Press an arrow key to move the point of focus (the active cell) one cell per click, in the direction of that arrow

2 Hold down the Ctrl key and press the arrow key, to move to the start or end of a range of data (an adjacent set of occupied cells)

3 To select cells while scrolling to the start or end of a range, hold down the Ctrl and Shift keys and press the arrow key

4 Press Ctrl+Shift+Arrow again to extend the selection

Scroll Lock

If you press the Scroll Lock button, to turn on scroll locking, this will change the actions performed by the arrow keys.

1 The arrow key now moves the window view up or down one row, or sideways one column, depending which arrow key you use (the location of the active cell is not changed)

2 Press Ctrl+Arrow key to shift the view vertically, by the depth of the window, or horizontally, by the width of the window, depending on the arrow key direction you choose

Scroll Bars

1 Click the vertical scroll arrows, to move one row up or down

2 Click above or below the scroll box, to move a window's depth up or down

3 Click the horizontal scroll arrows, to move one column to the left or right

4 Click to the left or right of the horizontal scroll box, to move a window width left or right

5 Click one of the scroll boxes, Excel displays the row number or column letter as you drag the box

Split View
You can split the window, so you can scroll separate parts of the worksheet in two or four panes, independently.

1 Hover over the split box on the vertical scroll bar, or the horizontal scroll bar

2 When the pointer becomes a double-headed arrow, click to display the split bar, drag this over the worksheet to where you want the split

Don't forget

The sizes of the scroll boxes are based on the ratios of visible data to total data, and their positions are the relative vertical and horizontal locations of the visible area within the worksheet.

45

Hot tip

To remove either the horizontal or vertical split bar, you just double-click on the bar.

Scroll with Wheel Mouse

1 Rotate the wheel forward or back, to scroll a few lines at a time

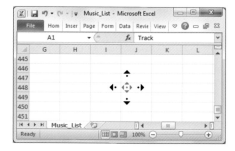

2 To change the amount scrolled, open Control Panel and select Mouse, then click the Wheel tab and change the number of lines, or select One screen at a time

Don't forget

The Wheel Mouse properties in Windows Vista also allow horizontal scrolling, if the wheel can be tilted left or right.

Continuous Scroll

1 Hold down the wheel button, then drag the pointer away from the origin mark, in the direction you want to scroll

2 Release the wheel when you reach the required position

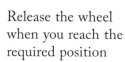

Hot tip

Move the pointer away from the origin mark to speed up scrolling. Move the pointer closer to the origin mark to slow down scrolling.

Hands-Free Scroll

1 To scroll automatically, click and release the wheel button, then move the mouse in the required direction

2 The further away from the origin mark you place the mouse pointer, the faster the scrolling

3 To slow down scrolling, move the mouse pointer back, closer to the origin mark

4 To stop automatic scrolling, click any mouse button

Navigate with Keystrokes

The use of the arrow keys for navigation is covered on page 44. Here are some additional keyboard shorts.

End Key

With Scroll Lock off, press End, then press one of the arrow keys, to move to the edge of the data region

With Scroll Lock on, press End to move to the cell in the lower-right corner of the window

Ctrl+End moves to the last used cell (end of lowest used row)

Ctrl+Shift+End extends the selection to the last used cell

Home Key

With Scroll Lock off, press Home, to move to the beginning of the current row

With Scroll Lock on, press Home, to move to the cell in the upper-left corner of the window

Ctrl+Home moves to the beginning of the worksheet

Ctrl+Shift+Home extends the selection to the beginning

Page Down Key

Page Down moves one screen down in the worksheet

Alt+Page Down moves one screen to the right

Ctrl+Page Down moves to the next sheet in the workbook

Ctrl+Shift+Page Down selects the current and next sheet

Page Up Key

Page Up moves one screen up in the worksheet

Alt+Page Up moves one screen to the left

Ctrl+Page Up moves to the previous sheet in the workbook

Ctrl+Shift+Page Up selects the current and previous sheet

Tab Key

Tab moves one cell to the right, in the worksheet

Shift+Tab moves to the previous cell in the worksheet

Don't forget

If you are entering or changing data, using the keyboard, you might prefer to stay on the keyboard and use these additional shortcuts to navigate the worksheet, rather than using the mouse.

Sort Rows

If you are looking for particular information, and don't know exactly where it appears in the worksheet, you can use Excel commands to help locate the items.

1 Click the column that contains the information, select Sort & Filter, from the Home tab, then Editing group

Don't forget

Custom Sort allows you to sort the worksheet by several fields, Artists and Albums for example.

2 Choose Sort A to Z (or Sort Z to A, if the required information would be towards the end of the list)

Hot tip

Excel will sort the rows of data, using the column selected, so all the related data will stay together.

3 Scroll through the list (using the navigation techniques described on pages 44–45) to locate the relevant entries

4 Click No when you close the workbook, to preserve the original sequence of entries

Don't forget

Excel provides a more structured way of handling a range of data like this, with the Excel Table – see page 72.

Find Entries

If you'd rather not change the sequence of the rows, you can use the Find command to locate appropriate entries.

1 Click the column with the information, choose Find & Select, from the Editing group on the Home tab, then click Find (or press Ctrl+F)

Don't forget

Select all the cells in the column, the search will be restricted to that part of the worksheet.

2 Click the Options button, if necessary (Excel remembers the last setting)

3 Specify a word or phrase, select the options, to search within the worksheet and in the Column, and then click Find Next

Hot tip

You can include case in the check, and you can require a full match with the entire cell contents.

4 Repeat Find Next, to locate subsequent matching entries

5 You can click Find All to get a list of the cell addresses for matching entries

Filter Information

The Filter part of the Sort & Filter command can be very helpful in assessing the information you have imported, because it allows you to concentrate on particular sections of the data.

1 Select all the data (for example, click in the data region, press Ctrl+End, then press Shift+Ctrl+Home)

Don't forget

If there's only one block of data, you can press Ctrl+A to select all the cells in the worksheet.

2 Select Sort & Filter from the Home tab, Editing group, and then click the Filter command

3 Click the arrow box in the column heading, to display unique values

Hot tip

If you want just a few entries, clear the (Select All) box, which clears all the boxes, then just reselect the ones you want.

4 Clear the boxes for unwanted values, to leave those you want to view, e.g. guest artists

5 Click the OK button, to display the required entries

6 Make the changes that are required (e.g. copy guest artists to the Comments field, leaving just the main artist)

Hot tip

Having consistent values for the entries makes it much easier to sort and organize your information.

7 Click the arrow on the header, to see the revised list of unique values

8 Click (Select All), and then click OK to redisplay all the entries

Don't forget

To remove the filters from all columns, reselect the Filter command, from the Home tab, Editing group. All entries will then be displayed.

You can filter for blank entries, to identify cells with missing data.

1 Click the arrow for Track, click (Select All) to clear the box, then select (Blanks) and 32, then click OK

Hot tip

In this view of the worksheet, columns D to H are hidden (see page 55), to make it easier to view the relevant sections of data.

2 You can then correct the missing entries, in this case, by copying the track numbers from the FileName column

Remove Duplicate Entries

A duplicate entry is where all values in the row are an exact match for all the values in another row.

To find and remove duplicate values:

1 Select the range of cells

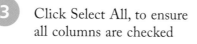

2 Select the Data tab, then, from the Data Tools group, click Remove Duplicates

3 Click Select All, to ensure all columns are checked

4 Clear the box for "My data has headers", if you suspect these may be repeated

5 Click OK, to detect and delete the duplicates

A message is displayed, indicating how many duplicate values were removed and how many unique values remain

6 Click OK

There's no Undo for this operation – the duplicates have been permanently removed.

Check Spelling

A spelling check is sometimes a useful way to assess the contents of some sections of your worksheet.

 1 Select the relevant parts: for example, click one column, press and hold Ctrl, then click more columns

Don't forget

Choose columns of data that are suitable for spell-checking.

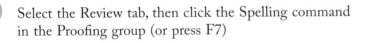

2 Select the Review tab, then click the Spelling command in the Proofing group (or press F7)

3 Click Change All, if the word being corrected is likely to appear more than once

4 Click Ignore All, if there are spelling warnings for valid terms or foreign words

5 Click OK when the spelling check is complete

Freeze Headers and Labels

When you navigate a worksheet, column headings and row labels will move off screen, making it more difficult to identify the data elements. To keep these visible, start by clicking on the worksheet.

1 Click the cell below the headings and to the right of the labels (e.g. with one row and one column, choose cell B2)

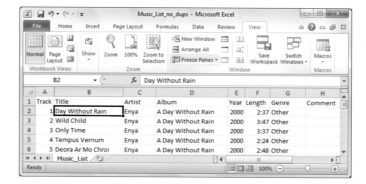

2 Select the View tab and click the Freeze Panes command, from the Window group

3 Choose the appropriate option from the list

4 The first entry for the Freeze Panes command changes to the undo option, Unfreeze Panes

Hide Columns or Rows

To make it easier to view particular portions of the worksheet, you can tell Excel not to display certain columns or rows

1 Select the columns or rows that you want to hide. For example, to select non-adjacent columns, select the first column, hold down Ctrl, then select subsequent columns

Hot tip

You cannot cancel the selection of a cell, or range of cells in a non-adjacent selection, without canceling the entire selection.

2 Select the Home tab, then click the Format command from the Cells group

3 Select Hide & Unhide, then click Hide Columns or Hide Rows, as required

Don't forget

A column or row also becomes hidden, if you change its column width or row height to zero. The Unhide command will reveal columns and rows hidden in this way.

To redisplay the hidden rows or columns:

1 Select the rows above and below hidden rows, or select the columns either side of hidden columns

2 Open the menu and select Unhide Columns or Rows

Hot tip

You can also right-click the selected columns or rows, and then click Hide or Unhide from the menu that appears.

Protect a Worksheet

1 Select any column (e.g. Comments) that you might want to update

2 On the Home tab, select Format from the Cells group, then click Format cells

3 Select the Protection tab, then clear the Locked box, and the Lock Text box also, if this is displayed

4 To protect the remaining part of the worksheet, select Format again, and this time select Protect Sheet

5 Ensure that all users are allowed to select locked and unlocked cells, then click OK

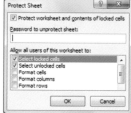

6 You can edit cells in the chosen columns, but you will get an error message if you try to edit any other cells

4 Formulas and Functions

Various formats for numbers are explained, and options for referencing cell locations are reviewed. These provide the basis for an introduction to functions and formulas, beginning with operators and calculation sequence, including formula errors and cell comments.

Number Formats

The values can be typed
directly into the cells,
imported from another
application (see page 42),
or created by a formula.

Don't forget

The cells in the worksheet contain values, in the form of numbers
or text characters. The associated cell formats control how the
contents are displayed.

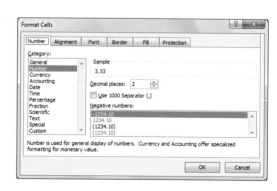

Cells B2 to B10 all contain the same value (3.33333) but each cell
has a different format, which changes the way the number appears
on the worksheet. To set the number format:

Don't forget

You can also open Format
Cells from the Home tab,
by clicking the arrow in
the Font group.

1. Select the cell or cells, then click the Home tab, select
Format, in the Cells group, and choose
Format Cells

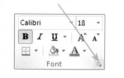

2. Select the Number tab and choose the
category, to see how the contents would
appear, and to select attributes, such as
decimal places and the appearance of
negative numbers

Don't forget

The default is General,
which is based on
the cell contents. Use
Number when you need
decimal places, and
Currency or Accounting
for money amounts.
The Special format is for
structured numbers, e.g.
zip or postal codes.

Date and Time are also number formats, but, in this case, the number is taken as the days since a base point in time.

Because dates and times are stored as numbers, you can use them in formulas and calculations.

Cells B3 to B6 are formatted as dates or times. The same numbers are shown in cells B8 to B11, formatted as General. This shows that day 1 is January 1st, 1900, and day 39100 is January 18th, 2007, while day 39107 is a week later. Decimals indicate part days.

To set or change the date or time format:

 Open Format Cells, select the Number tab, click Date or Time, to see the list of format options

Some of the formats depend on the specific country and locations defined in the Windows regional options, found in the Control Panel.

 Choose a format option and click OK, or click Custom to see other time and date formatting options

Text Formats

Excel recognizes cells containing text, such as header and label cells, and gives them the General format, with default text format settings (left-aligned, and using the standard font).

To change the format for such cells:

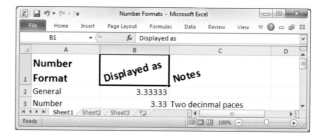

Hot tip

See page 30 for more examples on setting text format options for font and alignment, including the Merge Cells option.

1 Select the cells and open Format Cells, select the Font tab and choose the font, style, size, and color

Don't forget

The text in cell A1, as shown above, uses the Wrap Text option to keep the text within the column width. Cells B1 and C1 illustrate the use of Orientation, to fit the headings into the cells.

2 Select the Alignment tab and change the text controls, alignment, or orientation settings

Relative References

A cell could contain a formula, rather than an actual value. Excel performs the calculation the formula represents, and displays the result as the value for that cell. For example:

In this worksheet, cell D3 shows the amount spent on DVDs (price times quantity), calculated as =B3*C3.

The formulas for D4 and D5 are created by copying and pasting D3. The cell references in the formula are relative to the position of the cell containing them, and are automatically updated for the new location.

A cell reference in this form is known as a relative reference, and this is the normal type of reference used in worksheets.

The results of formulas can be used in other formulas, so the total in cell D6 is calculated as =D3+D4+D5.

The sales tax in cell D7 is calculated as =D6*B7. Note that B7 is displayed as a value of 7.5%, the cell format being Percentage. The actual value stored in the cell is 0.075.

The worksheet could have used a constant value instead, such as =D5*7.5/100 or =D5*7.5%. However, having the value stored in a cell makes it easier to adapt the worksheet when rates change. It also helps when the value is used more than once.

The shipping cost in cell D8 is a stored constant.

The final calculation in the worksheet is the total cost in cell D9, which is calculated as =D6+D7+D8.

Hot tip

The cells hold formulas as stored values, but it is the results that normally get displayed. To switch between results and formulas, press Ctrl+` (the grave accent key), or select the Formulas tab and click Show Formulas.

61

Don't forget

The value B7 is a relative cell reference, like the others, but this may not be the best option. See page 62 for the alternative.

Absolute References

Assume that calculation of the sales tax per line item is required. The value in cell E3 for the DVDs product would be =D3*B7.

You might be tempted to copy this formula down into cells E4 and E5, but, as you see here, the results would be incorrect, giving zero values, because the relative reference B7 would be incremented to B8 and then B9, both of which are empty cells.

The answer is to fix the reference to B7, so that it doesn't change when the formula is copied. To indicate this, you edit the formula, to place a $ symbol in front of the row and column addresses.

Copy this formula down into cells E4 and E5, the reference $B$7 doesn't change, so the results are correct. This form of cell reference is known as an absolute reference.

A cell reference with only part of the address fixed, such as $D3 or D$3, is known as a **mixed reference**.

Don't forget

To fix the column, place $ before the column letter. Likewise, to fix the row, put $ before the row number. The other part of the reference will change when the formula is copied.

Hot tip

Select a cell reference in a formula, and press F4 to cycle between relative, absolute, and mixed cell references.

Name References

Names provide a different way of referring to cells in formulas. To create a name for a cell or cell range:

1 Select the cell, or the group of cells, you want to name

2 Click the Name box, on the left of the Formula bar

3 Type the name that you'll be using to refer to the selection, then press Enter

4 Click the Formulas tab and select the Name Manager, in the Defined Names group, to view names in the workbook

Names create absolute references to cells or ranges in the current worksheet. They can be used in formulas, and, when these are copied, the references will not be incremented.

63

Don't forget

Names must start with a letter, underscore, or backslash. They can contain letters, numbers, periods, and underscores, but not spaces, and case is ignored. Their maximum length is 255 characters.

Don't forget

Names can be defined for a cell, for a range or group of cells, or for constants and functions.

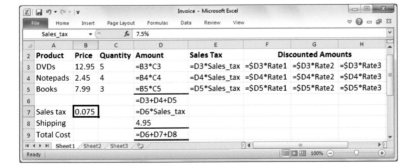

You cannot use certain names, such as R1, R2, R3, since these are actual cell references. You must specify non-ambiguous names, such as Rate1, Rate2, Rate3.

Operators

The formulas shown so far have used several operators (+, *, %), but there are many other operators you might use, in a number of categories, including the following:

Don't forget

Operators can be applied to constants, cell references, or functions.

Don't forget

The results of any of these comparisons will be a logical value, either True or False.

Hot tip

The Intersection of two ranges is a reference to all the cells that are common between the two ranges.

Category	Meaning	Examples
Arithmetic		
+ (plus sign)	Addition	A7+B5
- (minus sign)	Subtraction Negation	C6-20 -C3
* (asterisk)	Multiplication	C5*C6
/ (forward slash)	Division	C6/D3
% (percent sign)	Percent	20%
^ (caret)	Exponentiation or Power	D3^2
Comparison		
= (equal)	Equal to	A1=B1
> (greater than)	Greater than	A1>B1
< (less than)	Less than	A1<B1
>= (greater than with equal)	Greater than or equal	A1>=B1
<= (less than with equal)	Less than or equal	A1<=B1
<> (not equal)	Not equal	A1<>B1
Text		
& (ampersand)	Connect/join	"ABCDE"&"FGHI"
Reference		
: (colon)	Range	B5:B15
, (comma)	Union	SUM(B5:B15,D5:D15)
(space)	Intersection	B2:D6 C4:F8

Calculation Sequence

The order in which a calculation is performed may affect the result. As an example, the calculation 6+4*2 could be interpreted in two different ways. If the addition is performed first, this would give 10*2, which equals 20. However, if the multiplication is performed first, the calculation becomes 6+8, which equals 14.

To avoid any ambiguity in calculations, Excel evaluates formulas by applying the operators in a specific order. This is known as **operator precedence**. The sequence is as follows:

Don't forget

Operator precedence is a mathematical concept used by all programming languages and applications, such as spreadsheet programs that include computation.

1	: ▢ ,	Colon Space Comma
2	-	Negation
3	%	Percentage
4	^	Expenential
5	* /	Multiplication Division
6	+ -	Addition Subtraction
7	&	Concatenation
8	= < > <= >= <>	Comparison

When the formula has several operators with the same precedence, multiplication and division for example, Excel evaluates the operators from left to right.

These are some example formulas that illustrate the effect of operator precedence on the calculation result:

	A	B	C
1	=4+6*3	22	Multiplication then addition
2	=(4+6)*3	30	Addition in parentheses then multiplication
3	=4+6/2*3	13	Division then multiplication then addition
4	=(4+6)/(2*3)	1.666666667	Multiplication then addition then division
5	=((4+6)/2)*3	15	Addition then division then multiplication

Microsoft Excel - Precedence A7 fx
Sheet1 Sheet2 Sheet3 Ready 100%

You can use parentheses to change the order of evaluation, since expressions within parentheses will be evaluated first. If there are parentheses within parentheses (nested), Excel will evaluate the expression in the innermost pair of parentheses first, and work out towards the outermost.

Functions

Functions are predefined formulas that perform calculations based on specific values, called arguments, provided in the required sequence. The function begins with the function name, followed by an opening parenthesis, the arguments for the function separated by commas, and a closing parenthesis. They are used for many types of calculation, ranging from simple to highly complex.

If you are unsure which function is appropriate for the task, Excel will help you search for the most appropriate. To select a function in the Invoice worksheet:

1 Click the cell where you want to use a function as the formula, the total amount cell D6 for example.

2 Click Insert Function, on the Formula bar

3 Enter the phrase Total numbers in the Search for a function box, and click Go to list related functions

4 Select the most appropriate function, in this case SUM, and click OK

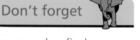
5 Review the arguments, in this case range D3:D5, see the answer this gives, and click OK, if this is as expected

Autocomplete

Even when you know the function needed, Excel will help you set it up, to help avoid possible syntax and typing errors.

1 Click the worksheet cell, and begin typing the function, for example, click the total cost cell D9 and type =s

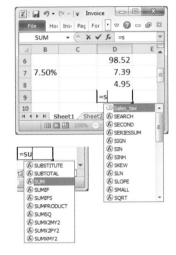

2 Excel lists functions that match so far, so you can select a function and see its description, scroll down to see more names, or continue typing, for example =su, to narrow the list

3 When you find the function that you require, double-click the name, then enter the arguments that are shown

4 For example, click D6, press period, and click D8

5 Type the closing parenthesis, and then press Enter

6 The formula with the function is stored in the cell, and the result of the operation will be displayed

As always, you should save the spreadsheet from time to time, to preserve the changes you make.

Hot tip

Click on the function name in the prompt, to display help for that function.

67

Don't forget

Type the range name, if you have already defined the required cells (see page 63).

AutoSum

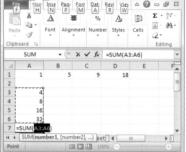

1 Select the cell below a column of numbers

Hot tip

All the cells up or across, to the first non-numeric or empty cell, are included in the total.

2 To total the numbers, click AutoSum, in the Editing group on the Home tab

3 Press Enter, or click on the tick in the Formula bar, to add the function

4 Similarly, select the cell to the right of a row of numbers and click AutoSum to total them

Hot tip

In either case, you can click the arrow next to AutoSum, and select from the list of functions offered to automatically add a different function.

When the selected cell could be associated with a row or a column, AutoSum will usually favor the column. However, you can adjust the direction or extent of the range in the formula before you apply it to the worksheet.

The same AutoSum option is also provided in the Function Library group, on the Formulas tab, along with links to various sets of functions.

68

Formula Errors

Excel helps you to avoid some of the more common errors when you are entering a formula.

 1   When you type a name, Excel outlines the associated cell or range, so you can confirm that it is the correct selection

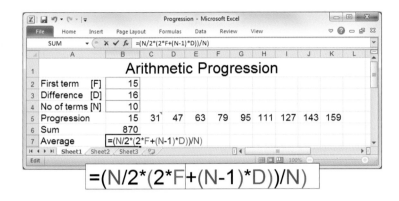

$$=(N/2*(2*F+(N-1)*D))/N)$$

2   With nested functions, Excel colors the parentheses, to help you ensure that they are in matching open/close pairs

3   If you do make an error, such as the extra parenthesis shown above, it is often detected and corrected

4   If the result overflows the available space, Excel displays hash signs

5   There's a similar display for other errors, but, in addition, a green flash shows in the top left-hand corner of the cell.

6   Select the cell, then click the information icon and the Help entry, for more details

69

Add Comments

You can add notes to a cell, perhaps to explain the way in which a particular formula operates.

 Click the cell where the comment is meant to appear

 Select the Review tab, and click New Comment, in the Comments group

 Your user name is shown, but you can delete this if you wish, then add your comments

> Michael Price:
> =if(count($B5:B5)<N,B5+D," ")
> This formula displays the next number in the series, until the required N terms have been displayed, then it displays a blank. It is copied into the cells to its right.

31   159

 Format the text, if desired, and then click outside the comment box to finish

> C5 f_x =IF(COUNT($B5:B5)<N,B5+D," ")
>
> ## Arithmetic Progression
>
> | | A | B | C |
> |---|---|---|---|
> | 2 | First term [F] | 15 | |
> | 3 | Difference [D] | 16 | |
> | 4 | No of terms [N] | 10 | |
> | 5 | Progression | 15 | 31 |
> | 6 | Sum | 870 | |
> | 7 | Average | 87 | |
>
> Michael Price:
> =if(count($B5:B5)<N,B5+D," ")
> This formula displays the next number in the series, until the required N terms have been displayed, then it displays a blank. It is copied into the cells to its right.
>
> 159
>
> Cell C5 commented by Michael Price

 The presence of a comment is indicated by the red flash at the top right of the cell, and the comment box appears when you move the mouse over the cell

 The Edit Comment command replaces the New Comment command, when the selected cell contains an existing comment

5 Excel Tables

The Excel table structure helps you to keep sets of data separate, so that you don't accidentally change other data when you are inserting or deleting rows and columns. There are other benefits also, such as structured cell references, automatic filters, sorts, and subtotals.

Create an Excel Table

To make it easier to manage and analyze a group of related data, you can turn a range of cells into an Excel Table. The range should contain no empty rows or columns.

To illustrate this feature, a table is used to interpret the genre (music classification) codes contained in the MP3 tags for music files (see page 40). This field often appears as a genre code, such as (2) for country music, or (4) for disco.

You can find a table of genre codes and meanings on the Internet, on web pages like www.true-audio.com/ID3#Genres:

![TAU Software - ID3~Genres - True Audio Codec Software - Windows Internet Explorer showing a Genres table with Genre ID # and Genre columns: 0 Blues, 1 Classic Rock, 2 Country, 3 Dance, 4 Disco]

1 Select the table in Internet Explorer, and press Ctrl+C

2 Open the Music_List worksheet, locate an empty column (leaving a space between it and the existing data)

3 Select the first cell in the column, and then press Ctrl+V to copy the Internet table of codes into the worksheet

![Music_List_no_dups - Microsoft Excel spreadsheet showing columns Track, Title, Artist, Genre, Status, and GenreID#/Genre. Rows: 1 Day Without Rain Enya -12 OK; 2 Wild Child Enya -12 OK; 3 Only Time Enya -12 OK; 4 Tempus Vernum Enya -12 OK; 5 Deora Ar Mo Chroi Enya -12 OK; 6 Flora's Secret Enya -12 OK; 7 Fallen Embers Enya -12 OK; 8 Silver Inches Enya -12 OK; 9 Pilgrim Enya -12 OK. GenreID# column: 0 Blues, 1 Classic Rock, 2 Country, 3 Dance, 4 Disco, 5 Funk, 6 Grunge, 7 Hip-Hop, 8 Jazz]

4 With the data selected, click the Insert tab, then click Table in the Tables group

5 Check that the appropriate range of data is selected

6 If the first row has names, click "My table has headers"; otherwise, let Excel generate default headers

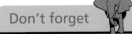

73

The table is given the default banding style, and Filter boxes are automatically added in the header row of each column, allowing you to sort or filter the contents.

The table will be given a default name, such as Table1. To change this name:

1 Click in the table, and click the Design tab

2 Click the Table Name box in the Properties group, to highlight the name

3 Type a new name for the table, Code for example, and press Enter to apply the change (and update references to the old table name)

 page 63).

Edit Tables

1 Select the Music data, click Table, on the Insert tab, to create a table, and change its name to Music

2 Click on any column in the Music table that is not required, then select Home, click the arrow next to Delete in the Cells group, and choose Delete Table Columns

3 Go to the end of the Codes table, click in the last cell, and press Tab to add a row

4 Type an entry, such as 148, New, then add another row with 149, New and another with 150, Other

5 Select the cells with values 148 and 149, then select the Home tab, and choose Delete, Table Rows.

You'll find that inserting or deleting rows and columns in one table will not affect the other tables in the worksheet.

Table Styles

The Design tab provides options to change the formatting of the rows and columns in the table.

1 Specify if there's a header row, and turn banding on or off, using settings in the Table Style Options group

2 Click the Quick Styles button, in the Table Styles group, to view the full list of styles

3 The styles selection bar is displayed, if there's room on the ribbon, and you can scroll the styles, or press the More button to show the full list

4 Make changes to the Table Style Options, and the effects are incorporated into the Styles Selection panel

Table Totals

You can add a Totals row at the end of the table, and display the totals for columns (or use another function appropriate to the type of information stored in the column).

1 Click in the table, select the Design tab, and click the Total Row box in the Table Style Options group

The Subtotal function is inserted, with a number to indicate the operation:

101	AVERAGE
102	COUNT
103	COUNTA
104	MAX
105	MIN
106	PRODUCT
107	STDEV
108	STDEVP
109	SUM
110	VAR
111	VARP

Subtotal uses structured references to the table (see page 78).

2 The Totals row is added as the last row of the table, and the last column (BitRate) is given a Total

3 Select the Total cell, and click the arrow to see the Total function applied (in this case Count)

4 You can apply a Total to any column. For Title, Comment, and FilePath, you might use Count. For FileSize, perhaps Average is best. For Length, use Sum, and for Year, use Min or Max

The More Functions option allows any Excel function to be used for computing the total for that column.

Count Unique Entries

For Artist and Album, the ideal would be to count all unique entries, to give the numbers of individual artists and albums stored in the table. Here is one way to do this:

 1 Click in the Total cell for the Artist column, and begin typing the function =sum(1/countif(

 2 Click the Artist header, to extend the formula

 3 Type a comma, click the Artist header again, and then type two closing parentheses

4 This is an array formula, so press Shift+Ctrl+Enter (rather than Enter), and the count will be displayed

Hot tip

This calculates the frequency for each entry, inverts these counts, and sums up the resulting fractions. For example, if an entry appears three times, you get 1/3 + 1/3 + 1/3 for that entry, giving a count of 1. Each unique entry adds another 1.

Beware

This method of counting the number of duplicate entries assumes that there are no empty cells in the range being checked.

77

Don't forget

Use a similar formula to count the number of unique entries in the Album column.

Structured References

The formulas shown for the totals illustrate the use of structured references. These allow you to refer to the contents of a table, using meaningful names, without having to be concerned about the specific row numbers and column letters, or changes that are caused when rows and columns are added or deleted. The structured references use the table name and column specifiers:

=Music	The table data	A2: K479
=Music[Length]	All the data in the Length column	F2:F479

You can add a special item specifier, to refer to particular parts:

=Music[#All]	The entire table, with headers, data and totals	A1:K480
=Music[#Data]	The table data	A2:K479
=Music[#Headers]	The header row	A1:K1
=Music[#Totals]	The totals row	A480:K480
=[@Length]	The nth cell in the named column (where n is the active row)	Fn

Don't forget

Excel 2007 used Music [[#This Row],[Length]], but this is simplified in Excel 2010 to [@Length].

For formulas within the table, such as subtotals on the Totals row, you can leave off the table name. This forms an unqualified structured reference, e.g. [Bitrate]. However, outside the table, you need the fully qualified structured reference, e.g. Music[Bitrate].

Beware

You should avoid the use of special characters, such as space, tab, line feed, comma, colon, period, bracket, quote mark, or ampersand in your table and column names.

This formula includes two subtotal functions (see page 76) to obtain the minimum and the maximum values from the Bitrate column. The results are separated by a hyphen, and the three items are concatenated (joined), to form a single text string. This is displayed in the cell K334, which contains the formula.

Calculated Columns

You can add a calculated column to an Excel table. This uses a single formula that adjusts for each row, automatically expanding to include additional rows.

Start by inserting a new column in the table.

1 Click the end column (Bitrate), select the Home tab, and click the arrow next to Insert, which is found in the Cells group

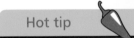

2 Click Insert Table Columns to the Right, and then rename the new column as Style (i.e. music style)

3 Click anywhere in the Style column and type a formula, then press Enter

4 The formula that you type is automatically filled into all cells of the column, above as well as below the active cell

---

Don't forget

You need to enter the formula only once, and you won't need to use the Fill or Copy command when the table grows.

Hot tip

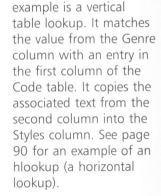

The formula in this example is a vertical table lookup. It matches the value from the Genre column with an entry in the first column of the Code table. It copies the associated text from the second column into the Styles column. See page 90 for an example of an hlookup (a horizontal lookup).

Insert Rows

1 Scroll to the last cell in the table, press Tab to add a new row, you'll see that the new formula is replicated

2 To add more data from a text file (see page 42), click a cell in an empty part of the worksheet, select the Data tab and From Text (in the Get External Data group)

3 Locate and double-click the data file, then use the Text Import Wizard to specify the structure of the data file

4 Confirm the temporary location for the data in the worksheet

...cont'd

5 Highlight the new data (excluding the header row), select the Home tab, and click Copy from the Clipboard group

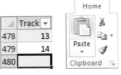

6 Click the first cell in the new row at the end of the table, then select Paste, from the Clipboard group

7 Additional rows are inserted into the table, to accommodate the new data records

> **Microsoft Excel**
>
> This table inserted rows into your worksheet. This may cause data in cells below the table to shift down.
>
> ☐ Do not display this dialog again
>
> [OK]

8 The data rows are inserted into the extended table

9 The Totals are automatically adjusted, and you'll see that Style, the calculated column, is extended to display values for the new data rows

81

Hot tip

You can type new rows directly into the table, pressing tab at the end of each row, ready to enter the next row.

Beware

Adding new rows or columns to the table causes worksheet data outside the table to be shifted. You should check for potential problems in data that is not in a defined table.

Don't forget

When the rows have been inserted, you can delete the temporary data stored in the worksheet below the table.

Custom Sort

When new rows are inserted, it may be appropriate to sort the table, to position the new rows where they belong.

1 Click in the table, select the Home tab, click Sort & Filter, in the Editing group, and select Custom Sort

Or

Click in the table, select the Data tab, and click Sort, in the Sort & Filter group

2 The first time, there are no criteria defined, so click the arrow in "Sort by" to add a header, e.g. Artist

3 Click the Add Level button, choose a second header (e.g. Album), and then add a third level (Track) and click OK

Print a Table

You can print a table without having to select the print area explicitly (see page 32).

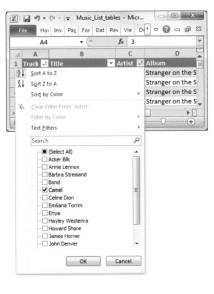

1 Select any cell in the table to activate it

2 Use Filters to restrict the display and print, for example, music for a specific Artist

3 Press the File tab, and then select Print (or press the shortcut key Ctrl+P)

4 For Settings, choose Print Selected Table, then adjust the paper size and scaling, if needed

5 Specify the number of copies required, then click the Print button to complete the process

Print

Hot tip

You may wish to change to a different table style, one more suitable for printing (or select None for a plain effect).

Don't forget

You can print the active worksheet, the entire workbook, the selected data, or the active table.

Print Active Sheets
Only print the active sheets

Print Entire Workbook
Print the entire workbook

Print Selection
Only print the current selection

Print Selected Table
Only print the selected table

Ignore Print Area

Beware

Subtotals will be adjusted to match the filtered results. However, some formulas on the Totals row may continue to reference the whole of the table contents.

83

Summarize a Table

You can summarize the data, using the PivotTable feature. See page 165 for another example.

1 Click in the table, select the Insert tab, and then click the PivotTable button, in the Tables group

2 Choose the location for the PivotTable report, either a new worksheet or an empty portion of the current worksheet, and then click OK

3 An empty PivotTable report is added at that location

4 Click the boxes to select fields from the Field List (for example, Artist, Album, Track, and Length)

5 Rearrange the fields by clicking and dragging, or right-click a name and select the area where it should appear

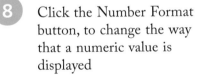

6 Click a numeric field in the Values list to reposition, move to a different area, or change value field settings

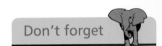

7 Choose how to summarize the values (e.g. sum, count, or average them)

8 Click the Number Format button, to change the way that a numeric value is displayed

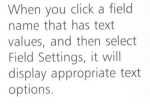

9 When you select PivotTable, Design and Options commands will be added to the Ribbon

Don't forget

When you click a field name that has text values, and then select Field Settings, it will display appropriate text options.

85

Hot tip

Click the Field List toggle command in the Show/ Hide group, to hide or reveal the field list. From here, you can also collapse or expand the report details.

Convert to a Range

You can turn an Excel table back into a range of data.

1 Click in the table to display the Table Tools entry on the ribbon

Table Tools
Design

Summarize with PivotTable
Remove Duplicates
Convert to Range
Tools

2 Select the Design tab, then click Convert to Range in the Tools group

3 Click Yes, to confirm that you do want to convert the table to a data range

Microsoft Excel

Do you want to convert the table to a normal range?

Yes   No

4 The cell styles will be preserved, but the filter boxes will be removed from the headers

	A	B	C	D	E	F	G	H	I
1	Track	Title	Artist	Album	Year	Length	Genre	Comment	FilePath
2		1 Stranger On The Shore	Acker Bill	Stranger on the Shore	1992	00:02:51	-12		C:\Users\I
3		2 Hey Jude	Acker Bill	Stranger on the Shore	1992	00:04:09	-12		C:\Users\I
4		3 Ramblin' Rose	Acker Bill	Stranger on the Shore	1992	00:02:45	-12		C:\Users\I
5		4 Jean	Acker Bill	Stranger on the Shore	1992	00:02:52	-12		C:\Users\I

Music_List_tables - Microsoft Excel
File Home Insert Page Layout Formulas Data Review View
A55 = 1
Music_List
Ready

5 The Totals row will still appear, but all references will now be standard $A$1-style absolute cell references

	A	B	C	D	E	F	G	H	I
532		10 Until You Come Back	Whitney	My Love Is Your Love	1998	00:04:52	-12		C:\Users\I
533		11 I Bow Out	Whitney	My Love Is Your Love	1998	00:04:30	-12		C:\Users\I
534		12 You'll Never Stand Alo	Whitney	My Love Is Your Love	1998	00:04:20	-12		C:\Users\I
535		13 I Was Made to Love Hi	Whitney	My Love Is Your Love	1998	00:04:25	-12		C:\Users\I
536	Total		534	21		43	1975	07:08:44	13	5

Music_List_tables - Microsoft Excel
File Home Insert Page Layout Formulas Data Review View
B536 = =SUBTOTAL(103,Music_List!$B$2:$B$535)
Music_List
Ready

6 If you convert the range into a table again, you will need to recreate the structured reference formulas for the Totals row and the calculated columns

6 Advanced Functions

There is a large library of functions. To help locate the ones you want, related functions are grouped by category, and there's a Recently Used list. More functions are provided via Excel Add-ins. With nested functions in your formulas, use the Evaluate command to see how they work.

Function Library

1 Select the Formulas tab to see the Function Library group, with a Ribbon style that depends on window size

Hot tip

The Function Library contains almost 400 functions, so categories are used to organize them, and there's also a search facility.

This starts with the Insert Function command, which allows you to enter keywords to search for a function (see page 66). It provides the syntax, and a brief description for any function that you select, plus a link to more detailed help. Alternatively, you can select from one of the categories.

2 Click a Category command, for an alphabetical list of the names of the functions that are included

The categories, and the number of functions included in each, are:

AutoSum	5	Math & Trig	63
Recently Used	10	More Functions	
Financial	53	Statistical	98
Logical	7	Engineering	41
Text	24	Cube	7
Date & Time	22	Information	17
Lookup & Ref	18	Compatibility	38

AutoSum

AutoSum (introduced on page 68) provides quick access to functions (Sum, Average, Count, Min and Max) that are likely to be the most frequently used functions in many workbooks.

Recently Used

Recently Used remembers the functions you last used, allowing you to make repeated use of functions, with the minimum of fuss, without having to remember their particular categories.

Don't forget

AutoSum and Recently Used are the only categories that include duplicates of functions.

Logical Functions

Sometimes the value for one cell depends on the value in another cell. For example, test scores could be used to set grade levels.

Hot tip

Comparisons (e.g. using the $<$, $=$, or $>$ operators) that are either True or False are the basis of logical functions.

 The formula in C2 is =B2>=50 and gives the result True or False, depending on the value in B2

 To display the more meaningful Pass or Fail, you'd use an IF formula, such as in D2, with =IF(B2>=50,"Pass","Fail")

Don't forget

The AND function includes a set of logical tests, all of which must be True, to give a True result.

3 Sometimes you need to check two conditions, e.g. in the E3 formula =IF(AND(B3>=50,B4>=50),"Merit","n/a")

The IF functions can be nested, with the False value being replaced by another IF function, to make a further test.

 This formula gives the country code, if the name matches, or goes on to test for the next country name in the list

Hot tip

You could use an OR function for the first two countries here, since a match for either would give the same code.

Lookup/Reference Functions

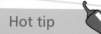

If you have a number of items to check against, set up a list.

1 This example uses a list of country names (in alphabetical order), with their country codes stored in rows D1:IF2

2 The range is named IDC

3 The lookup function requires the value, the lookup range, and the row number for the result (in this case row 2)

4 Copy the formula down, to check other country names

5 A mistype of Andorra results in N/A, indicating that no match could be found

To reverse the process, and replace a number with a text value, you could use the CHOOSE function. For example:

1 To convert the value in cell B2 into a Rank, enter
=CHOOSE(B2,"First","Second","Third","Fourth","Fifth")

	A	B	C	D	E	F	G
1		Tom	Dick	Harry	Yvonne	Khan	
2	Position	3	5	2	1	4	
3	Rank	Third	Fifth	Second	First	Fourth	

B3 ▾ fx =CHOOSE(B2,"First","Second","Third","Fourth","Fifth")

2 Copy the formula across to rank cells C2 to F2

3 To apply a suffix to the position value, use the formula
=B2&CHOOSE(B2,"st","nd","rd","th","th")

B4 ▾ fx =B2&CHOOSE(B2,"st","nd","rd","th","th")

	A	B	C	D	E	F	G
1		Tom	Dick	Harry	Yvonne	Khan	
2	Position	3	5	2	1	4	
3	Rank	Third	Fifth	Second	First	Fourth	
4	Standing	3rd	5th	2nd	1st	4th	

4 Copy the formula across to rank cells C2 to F2

You can store the values in a range of cells, but you must list the relevant cells individually.

B6 ▾ fx =CHOOSE(B2,$H$1,$H$2,$H$3,$H$4,$H$5)

	A	B	C	D	E	F	G	H
1		Tom	Dick	Harry	Yvonne	Khan		Top
2	Position	3	5	2	1	4		Runner Up
3	Rank	Third	Fifth	Second	First	Fourth		Also Ran
4	Standing	3rd	5th	2nd	1st	4th		Finished
5								Finished
6	Status	Also Ran	Finished	Runner Up	Top	Finished		

You should use absolute cell references for the list of values, so that you can copy the formula without changing the references.

Hot tip

The contents of B2 are used as an index, to select from the list of 5 values provided. A maximum of 254 values could be used.

Hot tip

Here, the suffix chosen from the list is appended to the index number.

91

Beware

Index values outside the range provided (in these examples, 1–5) will cause a #Value! error.

Financial Functions

Excel includes specialized functions for dealing with investments, securities, loans, and other financial transactions. For example, to calculate the monthly payments required for a mortgage, you'd use the PMT function. To illustrate, assume a purchase price of $250,000, interest at 6% per annum, and a 30-year period:

1 Enter the initial information into a worksheet, then, for the payment, begin typing the function =PMT(

	A			D	E
		PMT(rate, nper, pv, [fv], [type])			
1	Purchase Price	Interest Rate	Duration	Payments/Year	Payment
2	250000	6.00%	30	12	=PMT(

Microsoft Excel - Mortgage — =PMT(

2 Click the Insert Function button, to display the input form for the function arguments

Function Arguments

PMT

Rate	B2/D2	= 0.005
Nper	C2*D2	= 360
Pv	A2	= 250000
Fv		= number
Type		= number

= -1498.876313

Calculates the payment for a loan based on constant payments and a constant interest rate.

Pv is the present value: the total amount that a series of future payments is worth now.

Formula result = ($1,498.88)

Help on this function

3 In the Rate box, enter the interest rate per payment period B2/D2 (i.e. 6%/12). In the Nper box, enter C2*D2 (30*12). In the PV box, enter A2 ($250,000). Click OK

Microsoft Excel - Mortgage — E2 — =PMT(B2/D2,C2*D2,A2)

	A	B	C	D	E
1	Purchase Price	Interest Rate	Duration	Payments/Year	Payment
2	250000	6.00%	30	12	($1,498.88)

Perhaps you'd like to know what would happen if you paid the mortgage off over a shorter period:

 1 Select the existing values and calculation, then drag down, using the Fill handle, to replicate into three more rows

	A	B	C	D	E
1	Purchase Price	Interest Rate	Duration	Payments/Year	Payment
2	250000	6.00%	30	12	($1,498.88)
3	250000	6.00%	25	12	($1,610.75)
4	250000	6.00%	20	12	($1,791.08)
5	250000	6.00%	15	12	($2,109.64)

E5 ▾ fx =PMT(B5/D5,C5*D5,A5)

 2 Change the duration to 25, 20 and 15 years, on successive rows, and observe the revised monthly payments required

3 Add a column, to show total interest paid, and enter the cumulative interest function =CUMIPMT(

93

YEARFRAC ▾ × ✓ fx =CUMIPMT(B2/D2,C2*D2,A2,1,C2*D2,0)

	A	B	C	D	E	F
1	Purchase Price	Interest Rate	Duration	Payments/Year	Payment	Total Interest
2	250000	6.00%	30	12	($1,498.88)	,1,C2*D2,0)
3	250000	6.00%				
4	250000	6.00%				
5	250000	6.00%				

Function Arguments

CUMIPMT

Rate	B2/D2	= 0.005
Nper	C2*D2	= 360
Pv	A2	= 250000
Start_period	1	= 1
End_period	C2*D2	= 360

= -289595.4726

Returns the cumulative interest paid between two periods.

End_period is the last period in the calculation.

Formula result = ($289,595.47)

Help on this function   OK   Cancel

The arguments are similar to those for PMT, with Type now mandatory (set it to 0, for payment at end of month). The result shows how much interest would be paid out.

Copy the formula down, to see the figures for the other loan durations.

F5 ▾ fx =CUMIPMT(B5/D5,

	C	D	E	F
1	Duration	Payments/Year	Payment	Total Interest
2	30	12	($1,498.88)	($289,595.47)
3	25	12	($1,610.75)	($233,226.05)
4	20	12	($1,791.08)	($179,858.64)
5	15	12	($2,109.64)	($129,735.57)

Date & Time Functions

Date and time values (see page 59) are numbers, and count the days since the starting point (usually January 1st, 1900). However, they can be displayed in various date or time formats.

Hot tip

Excel also supports the 1904 date system, the default for Apple Mac computers, where a date value of 1 is taken as January 2nd, 1904.

1 The whole-number portion of the value converts into month, day, and year (with account taken for leap years)

Don't forget

In the example, the value of the date is displayed, to illustrate the operations. You type the date, e.g. as 4/12/2007, and Excel automatically converts it into a number value, and then stores it in the cell. The cell format controls what's displayed.

2 The decimal portion indicates the time of day, so .123 is 2:57, and .765 is 6:21PM (or 18:21 on the 24-hour clock)

Date and Time Calculations

Beware

You can use date and time values in formulas, but, because of the calendar effects, the results may not always be what you'd expect.

B4	Difference in days
B5	Subtracts calendar day numbers (may be minus)
B6	Subtracts calendar months (may be minus)
B7	Difference in years (ignores the part year)
B8	Twelve months for every year +/- the difference in months
B9	Adding ten days to A3 gives Jan 4, 2008
B10	Adding ten work days (to allow for weekends and holidays) gives the later date Jan 8, 2008

There's a worksheet function called DateDif that's not listed in the Date & Time category, or shown in Excel Help. The syntax is:

=DATEDIF(StartDate,EndDate,Interval)

The Interval code controls the result the function produces:

Interval value	Calculates the number between the dates of
"y"	Whole years
"m"	Whole months
"d"	Days in total
"ym"	Whole months, ignoring the years
"yd"	Days, ignoring the years
"md"	Days, ignoring the months and years

When entering the Interval code into DateDif as a constant, you enclose it in quotes. However, if your interval code is stored in a worksheet cell, it should not be enclosed in quotes in the cell.

1 Use the DateDif function with each of these codes in turn, to calculate the difference between the dates stored in cells B15 and B16.

2 This function becomes useful when you need to calculate someone's exact age, in years, months, and days. For example, DateDif applied to the date of birth and the current date gives the following:

The & operators concatenate the results of the calculations, with the literal text values " years ", " months ", and " days".

95

Text Functions

Values can be presented in many different ways, even though they remain stored as numbers. Sometimes, however, you actually want to convert the values into text (enclosed in quotes), perhaps to include them in a specific format, in a report or message.

This uses the Text function. Its syntax is =TEXT(value, format).

1 Format a number as text, with a fixed number of decimal places, with a comma as the thousands separator, if desired

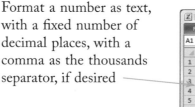

2 Display a number in money format, using any currency symbol

3 Display a number using the default currency for your system

4 Show the day of the week, for a date value, using the long or short form of the day name

5 For examples of the number formats, choose the Custom category, in the Format Cells dialog, and scroll the list

96

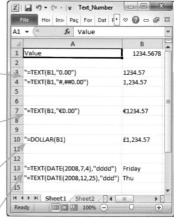

There are several functions provided to help you manipulate a piece of text, to make it more suitable for presentation.

1 Remove all extraneous blanks, leaving a single space between words

2 Convert all the characters in the text into lower-case format

	A	B
	fx The history of the New York sTOCK eXCHANGE	
1	The history of the New York sTOCK eXCHANGE	
2		
3	The history of the New York sTOCK eXCHANGE	=TRIM(A1)
4		
5	the history of the new york stock exchange	=LOWER(A3)
6		
7	The History Of The New York Stock Exchange	=PROPER(A5)
8		
9	The History Of The NYSE	=SUBSTITUTE(A7,"New York Stock Exchange","NYSE",1)

3 Convert all the text to proper case (title case)

4 Replace part of the text with different words

Excel does not have a Word Count function, but the text functions can be used in combination, to find the number of words in a cell.

	A	B
	fx =LEN(TRIM(A1))-LEN(SUBSTITUTE(A1," ",""))+1	
1	Mars, the red planet, is the fourth planet from the sun and the most Earth-like planet in our solar system. It is about half the size of Earth and has a dry, rocky surface and a very thin atmosphere. The surface of Mars is dry, rocky, and mostly covered with iron-rich dust. There are low-lying plains in the northern hemisphere, but the southern hemisphere is dotted with impact craters. The ground is frozen; this permafrost extends for several kilometers. The north and south poles of Mars are covered by ice caps composed of frozen carbon dioxide and water.	
2		
3	The number of words in the paragraph is	98

The Trim function removes multiple spaces from the text, then the first Len function counts all the characters, including spaces. The Substitute function removes all spaces from the text, then the second Len function counts the remaining characters. The difference between the two lengths is the number of spaces between words. Add one, and you will then have the number of words in the cell.

Math & Trig Functions

These functions allow you to carry out calculations, using cell contents, computed values, and constants.

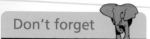
For example:

1 The Product function multiplies price times (1 – discount) quantity to get the cost of the item

2 Copy the formula, to calculate the costs for the other items

3 The total cost is the sum of the individual item costs

You may sometimes want to make calculations without showing all of the intermediate values.

For example:

1 The total cost (before discount) is the sum of the products of the item prices and item quantities, i.e. B3*D3 + B4*D4 + ...

2 This value is calculated with the Sumproduct function, which multiplies the sets of cells and totals the results

3 Rather than using the Sumproduct function to calculate the total discount, you can simply subtract actual cost from total cost. This avoids problems with rounding errors, which can show up in even straightforward functions, such as Sum. To illustrate the type of problem that can arise, imagine placing an order for goods where there's a special gift for spending $140 or more.

1 A quick check seems to indicate that the total is just over the amount required

2 But that the total Excel actually calculates is just under that amount

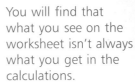

Excel hasn't got its sums wrong – the stored numbers that it totals aren't quite the same as those on display.

33.326667
13.326667
11.326667
9.266667
65.286667
7.460000
139.993333

3 Change the cell format, to show more decimal places, and you'll see the actual values are slightly lower than those shown

4 Click cell E3, and then add the Round function to the existing formula, to round the item cost to two places

5 Copy the formula into cells E4:E8, and you'll see that the total is now the expected amount

The Round function rounds up or down. So 1.234 becomes 1.23, while 1.236 becomes 1.24 (rounded to two decimal places). You can specify a negative number of places, to round the values to the nearest multiple of ten (-1 places) or of one hundred (-2 places), etc.

33.330000
13.330000
11.330000
9.270000
65.290000
7.460000
140.010000

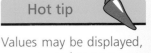
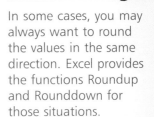

Random Numbers

It is sometimes useful to produce sets of random numbers. This could be for sample data, when creating or testing worksheets. Another use might be to select a variety of tracks from your music library, to generate a play list.

1 Click A1, and enter the function $=Rand()$, to generate a random number between 0 and 1

2 Copy A1 down into A2:A5, and a different number will be shown in each cell

3 Click C1 and enter function $=Randbetween(1,+10)$, which generates a whole number less than or equal to 10

4 Copy B1 down into B2:B5, and a number will be shown in each cell (with possible repeats, since there are only ten possibilities)

5 You can generate negative numbers: for example, E1:E5 has numbers between -99 and +99

6 Select the Formulas tab, click Calculate Now, in the Calculation group, and the numbers will change

Other Functions: Statistical

There's a large number of statistical functions, but the most likely one to be used is the Average function.

1 Create a block A1:E5 of random numbers between 101 and 200, to use as data for the functions

	A	B	C	D	E
1	139	147	135	128	123
2	125	128	126	174	115
3	177	163	126	113	110
4	162	185	158	124	189
5	169	126	121	120	108

Microsoft Excel - Stats
A1 — fx =RANDBETWEEN(101,200)

Hot tip

Use Copy, Paste Special, Paste Values, to replace the formulas, so that the set of random numbers generated won't later be affected by recalculation of the worksheet.

2 Define the name Sample for the range $A$1:$A$5

3 Select and Copy A1:E5, then select the Home tab, click the arrow on the Paste command, and select Paste Values (to replace the formula with the literal value, in each cell)

Calculate some typical statistics.

1 The arithmetic mean is =Average(Sample)

2 The number in the middle of the sample is =Median(Sample)

3 The most frequently occurring value is =Mode(Sample)

Stats - Microsoft ...
A1 — fx 139

	A	B	C	D	E
1	139	147	135	128	123
2	125	128	126	174	115
3	177	163	126	113	110
4	162	185	158	124	189
5	169	126	121	120	108
6					
7		=AVERAGE(Sample)			139.64
8		=MEDIAN(Sample)			128
9		=MODE(Sample)			126
10		=COUNT(Sample)			25
11		=COUNTIF(Sample,">=150")			8
12		=MAX(Sample)			189
13		=MIN(Sample)			108

Don't forget

There are a number of different ways to interpret the term Average. Make sure that you use the function that's appropriate for your requirements.

4 The number of values in the sample is =Count(Sample)

5 The number of values in the sample that are greater than or equal to 150 is =Countif(Sample,">=150")

6 The maximum value in the sample is =Max(Sample)

7 The minimum value in the sample is =Min(Sample)

Other Functions: Engineering

Hot tip

The Other Functions category also includes the Cube functions and Information functions.

There are some rather esoteric functions in the Engineering category, but some are quite generally applicable, for example:

 1 Convert from one measurement system to another, using the function =Convert(value, from_unit, to_unit)

	A	B	C	D
	Microsoft Excel - Stats			
C5			fx	'=CONVERT(CONVERT(1,"m","ft"),"m","ft")
1	0.832674185		=CONVERT(1,"pt","uk_pt")	Convert 1 US pint to UK pints
2	82.4		=CONVERT(28,"C","F")	Convert 28°C to °F
3	3600		=CONVERT(1,"pt","uk_pt")	Convert 1 hour to seconds
4	0.868976242		=CONVERT(1,"lbm","g")	Convert 1 pound to grams
5	10.76391042		=CONVERT(CONVERT(1,"m","ft"),"m","ft")	Convert 1 square meter to square feet

This function deals with units of weight and mass, distance, time, pressure, force, energy, power, magnetism, temperature, and liquids

There are functions to convert between any two pairs of number systems, including binary, decimal, hexadecimal, and octal.

 2 Convert decimal values to their binary, octal, and hexadecimal equivalents

	A	B	C	D	E
B19			fx	=DEC2BIN(A19)	
1	Decimal	Binary	Octal	Hexadecimal	Roman
2		=DEC2BIN(B2)	=DEC2OCT(B2)	=DEC2HEX(B2)	=ROMAN(B2)
3	0	0	0	0	
4	1	1	1	1	I
5	2	10	2	2	II
6	3	11	3	3	III
7	4	100	4	4	IV
8	5	101	5	5	V
9	6	110	6	6	VI
10	7	111	7	7	VII
11	8	1000	10	8	VIII
12	9	1001	11	9	IX
13	10	1010	12	A	X
14	11	1011	13	B	XI
15	12	1100	14	C	XII
16	13	1101	15	D	XIII
17	14	1110	16	E	XIV
18	15	1111	17	F	XV
19	16	10000	20	10	XVI

Don't forget

The function has an optional Form argument, to specify the Roman numeral style, the Classic style (0), or one of the more concise styles (1-4).

=ROMAN(1499,0)	MCDXCIX
=ROMAN(1499,1)	MLDVLIV
=ROMAN(1499,2)	MXDIX
=ROMAN(1499,3)	MVDIV
=ROMAN(1499,4)	MID

There's also a Roman numeral conversion, but it's just a one-way conversion between Arabic numerals and Roman numerals (and it comes from the Math & Trig category, rather than Engineering).

Excel Add-ins

There are Add-ins included with Excel, but they must be loaded before they can be used.

1 Click the File tab, and then click the Options button

2 Click the Add-Ins category, and, in the Manage box, click Excel Add-ins, and then click Go

3 To load the Excel Add-in, select the associated check-box, and then click OK

4 You may be prompted to install some of the add-in programs that you select

Data
Data Analysis
Solver
Analysis

Formulas
€ Euro Conversion
€ Euro Formatting
Off ▼
Solutions

5 The new functions can be found on the Formulas tab Solutions group, or on the Data tab Analysis group

Hot tip

If you are still looking for the functions you need, you may find them in an Excel Add-in, such as the Analysis ToolPak or the Solver Add-in.

Don't forget

To unload an Excel Add-in, clear the associated check-box, and then click OK. This does not delete the Add-in from your computer.

Evaluate Formula

If you are not sure exactly how a formula works, especially when there are nested functions, use the Evaluate command to run the formula one step at a time.

1 Select the cell with the formula you wish to investigate

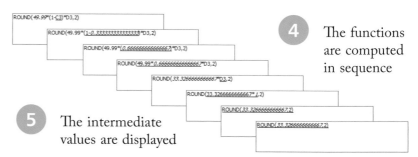

Hot tip

This is the formula for rounding the item costs, as shown in step 4 on page 99.

2 Select the Formulas tab, click the Formula Auditing button, and then select the Evaluate Formula command

Don't forget

Press the Step In button, to check details like the value of a constant, or to see the expansion of range or table names.

Click Step Out to carry on with the evaluation.

Click Restart, or Finish.

3 Press the Evaluate button, to move the calculation on a step, then press again to move to the subsequent steps

4 The functions are computed in sequence

5 The intermediate values are displayed

7 Control Excel

To keep control of your worksheets, audit the formulas, and check for errors. Make backup copies, and use the automatic save and recover capabilities. You can also control Excel through startup switches, shortcuts, KeyTips for the Ribbon commands, the Quick Access and Mini toolbars.

Audit Formulas

1 Click the Formulas tab, to see the Formula Auditing group

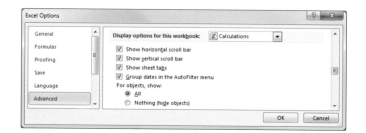

2 If the commands are grayed, click the File tab, select Excel Options, and then click Advanced

3 In the Display options for this Workbook section, make sure that the All option is selected

4 Select a cell, and click the Trace Precedents button in the Formula Auditing group

5 With cells where there is no formula such as B3, you receive a message

6 With cells, that contain a formula, such as E9, the arrow and box show the cells that are directly referred to by that formula

7 Click Trace Precedents, to see the next level of cells (if the first level of precedent cells refer to more cells)

8 Click Trace Dependents, to show the cells that rely on the value in the selected cell

9 Click Remove Arrows, in Formula Auditing

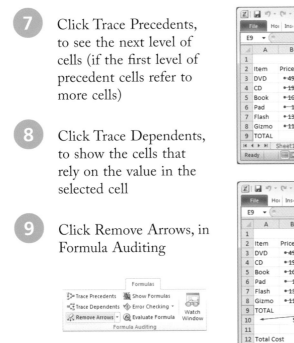

Don't forget

Dependents are those cells that contain formulas that refer to the selected cell.

You can analyze the role of cells that contain only literal values:

1 Click a cell, e.g. B2, that contains no formula, and click Trace Dependents

Microsoft Excel

⚠ The Trace Dependents command found no formulas that refer to the active cell.

[OK]

Was this information helpful?

2 If the cell isn't referred to by any formulas, you receive a warning message.

3 Select B3, and then click Trace Dependents three times, to view the cells that refer directly or indirectly to the selected cell

107

Protect Formulas

1 Click the Formulas tab, then click Show Formulas, to display the formulas in the worksheet

	A	B	C	D	E
7	Flash	13.99	0.333333333333333	7	=ROUND(B7*(1-C7)*D7,2)
8	Gizmo	11.19	0.333333333333333	1	=ROUND(B8*(1-C8)*D8,2)
9	TOTAL				=SUM(E3:E8)
10	=IF(E9>=140,"Special Gift Enclosed","Spend $140 to get that Special Gift")				
11					
12	Total Cost				=SUMPRODUCT(B3:B8,D3:D8)
13	Total discount				=E12-E9

A10 ▾ 𝑓ₓ =IF(E9>=140,"Special Gift Enclosed","Spend $140 to get that Special Gift")

2 Click Show Formulas again to return to displaying the results of the formulas

3 To hide a formula, select the cell, then click the Home tab, Format, and Format Cells

4 Click in the box labeled Hidden, and then click OK

Format Cells — Protection tab

☑ Locked
☑ Hidden

Locking cells or hiding formulas has no effect until you protect the worksheet (Review tab, Changes group, Protect Sheet button).

5 Click the Home tab, click Format, and select Protect Work Sheet, then click OK

Protect Sheet

☑ Protect worksheet and contents of locked cells
Password to unprotect sheet:

6 The formula will no longer display on the Formula bar when you select the cell. It is also hidden when you choose Show Formulas

	A	B	C	D	E
8	Gizmo	11.2	1/3	1	7.46
9	TOTAL				140.01
10			Special Gift Enclosed		
11					
12	Total Cost				209.99
13	Total discount				69.98

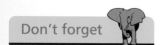

Check for Errors

Excel applies rules to check for potential errors in formulas.

1 Click the File tab, select Options, and then click Formulas

Excel Options

General	**Error Checking**
Formulas	☑ Enable background error checking
Proofing	Indicate errors using this color: [▼] [Reset Ignored Errors]
Save	
Language	**Error checking rules**
Advanced	☑ Cells containing formulas that result in an error ☑ Formulas which omit cells in a region
Customize Ribbon	☑ Inconsistent calculated column formula in tables ☑ Unlocked cells containing formulas
Quick Access Toolbar	☑ Cells containing years represented as 2 digits ☐ Formulas referring to empty cells
Add-Ins	☑ Numbers formatted as text or preceded by an apostrophe ☑ Data entered in a table is invalid
Trust Center	☑ Formulas inconsistent with other formulas in the region

[OK] [Cancel]

2 Select or clear the check-boxes, to change the errors that Excel will detect

3 Select Formulas, and click the arrow next to Error Checking, in the Formula Auditing group

Formulas

⧉ Trace Precedents   🔲 Show Formulas
⧉ Trace Dependents   ◈ Error Checking ▾
⧉ Remove Arrows ▾   ◈ Error Checking...
For   ◈ Trace Error
                       ⟲ Circular References ▾

4 Click Error Checking, to review errors one by one, making corrections on the Formula bar

Calculations - Microsoft Excel

File Home Insert Page Layout Formulas Data Review View

B1   ƒx =A1*2+1

	A	B	C	D	E	F	G
1		1	3	7	15	31	
2	31						
3							
4							
5							

Ready Circu

Error Checking

Error in cell B1
=A1*2+1

Formula Refers to Empty Cells

The formula in this cell refers to cells that are currently empty.

[Trace Empty Cell]
[Help on this error]
[Ignore Error]
[Edit in Formula Bar]

[Options...]   [Previous] [Next]

Error Checking

Error in cell C3
=SUM(A1toF1)

Invalid Name Error
The formula contains unrecognized text.

[Help on this error]
[Show Calculation Steps...]
[Ignore Error]
[Edit in Formula Bar]

[Options...]   [Previous] [Next]

5 Click the Next button, to review subsequent errors

Hot tip

Some errors will just be warnings, and some may be due to information not yet recorded.

Beware

If the worksheet has previously been checked, any Ignored errors will not appear until you press the Reset Ignored Errors button, in Excel Options.

...cont'd

You can also review individual errors on the worksheet.

1 Click an error, and then select Trace Error, from the Error Checking menu in Formula Auditing

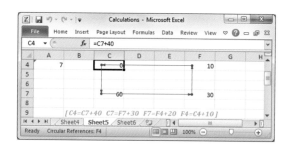

2 You can select Circular References, to see the cells that refer to their own contents, directly or indirectly

3 Click a cell from the list, to navigate to that location

4 Press F9 to recalculate the worksheet, and the cells involved in circular references will be identified

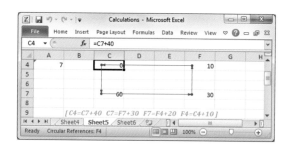

5 Click the Information button on an individual error, to see more options tailored to the particular error type

Backup

1 To make a copy of your workbook, click the File tab and select Open (or press the Ctrl+O shortcut key)

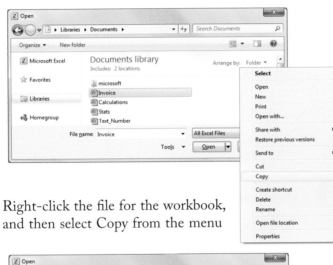

2 Right-click the file for the workbook, and then select Copy from the menu

3 Switch to the backup folder, right-click an empty area, and then select Paste

4 The file is copied to the folder, unless there's an existing copy in the backup folder

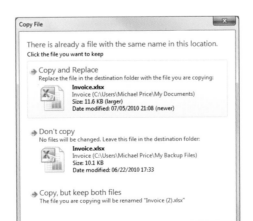

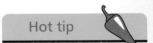

Hot tip

When you are working on a large worksheet, it is often helpful to make a copy before you apply significant changes, so that you can undo them, if necessary.

Don't forget

If there's already a copy, Windows compares the two versions, and lets you choose to replace the file, keep the two copies, or skip copying the workbook.

AutoSave and AutoRecovery

To review and adjust the AutoRecover and AutoSave settings:

1 Click the File tab, then click Options, and select Save

2 Make sure that the Save AutoRecover information box is checked, and adjust the frequency, if desired, then click OK to save any changes

If your system shuts down without saving the current changes, the next time you start up Windows and Excel, you'll be given the opportunity to recover your changes, as recorded up to the last AutoSave.

1 Click any of the entries, to review the contents, and Save the version of the file that contains the information you need

Startup Switches

When you start Excel normally, it displays the Excel splash screen, and then opens with a new blank workbook, e.g. Book1

To start Excel without these items displaying:

1 Press the Windows Logo key + R, type excel.exe /e, and then press Enter

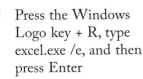

2 Excel opens without splash screen or workbook

When you start Excel, using the normal Start menu entry, these items will still be displayed.

Don't forget

You can use this method to start Excel in safe mode by typing excel.exe /safe. This can be useful if you are having problems opening a particular workbook.

113

Hot tip

You can create a shortcut to Excel, with your required parameters, and place this on the Start menu.

Create a Shortcut

To create a shortcut to Excel:

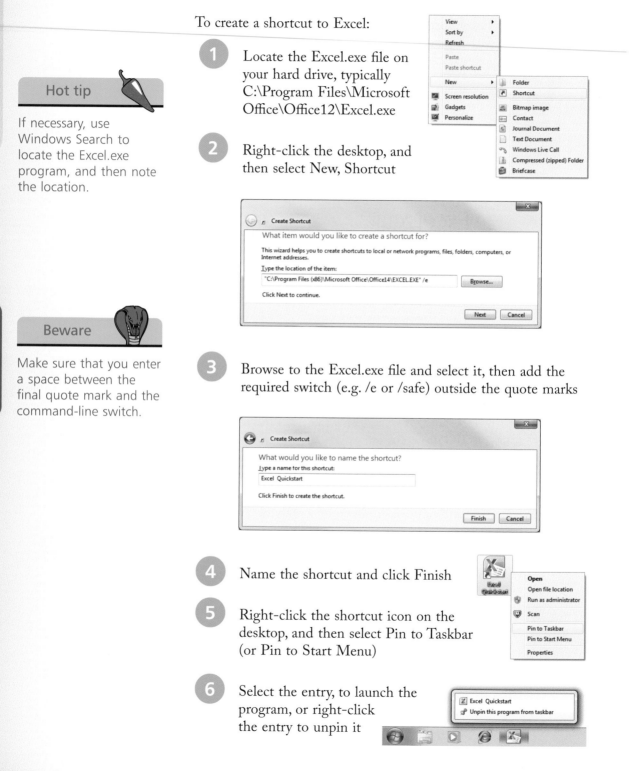

1 Locate the Excel.exe file on your hard drive, typically C:\Program Files\Microsoft Office\Office12\Excel.exe

2 Right-click the desktop, and then select New, Shortcut

Create Shortcut

What item would you like to create a shortcut for?

This wizard helps you to create shortcuts to local or network programs, files, folders, computers, or Internet addresses.

Type the location of the item:

"C:\Program Files (x86)\Microsoft Office\Office14\EXCEL.EXE" /e   Browse...

Click Next to continue.

Next   Cancel

3 Browse to the Excel.exe file and select it, then add the required switch (e.g. /e or /safe) outside the quote marks

Create Shortcut

What would you like to name the shortcut?

Type a name for this shortcut:

Excel Quickstart

Click Finish to create the shortcut.

Finish   Cancel

4 Name the shortcut and click Finish

Open
Open file location
Run as administrator
Scan
Pin to Taskbar
Pin to Start Menu
Properties

5 Right-click the shortcut icon on the desktop, and then select Pin to Taskbar (or Pin to Start Menu)

6 Select the entry, to launch the program, or right-click the entry to unpin it

Excel Quickstart
Unpin this program from taskbar

Ribbon KeyTips

Although the Ribbon is designed for mouse selection, it is still possible to carry out any task available on the Ribbon without moving your hands from the keyboard.

1 Press and release the Alt key (or press the F10 key) to show KeyTips (the keyboard shortcuts for the Ribbon)

2 Press the letter for the command tab that you want to display; for example, press W for View

3 Press the letter(s) for the command or group that you want; for example, press ZS for Show/Hide

115

Hot tip

If you hold down the Alt key for a couple of seconds, the KeyTips will display. Click F10 to hide them, temporarily.

Don't forget

The KeyTips change when you select a tab, and further KeyTips display when you select specific commands.

Hot tip

It doesn't matter if Alt is pressed or not: the shortcut keys in the KeyTips will still operate. You can also use upper or lower case.

Using KeyTips

 To go to a specific cell, C7 for example, press these keys:

You can go to a cell, using keystrokes only.

Alt

H

The action associated with a particular letter may change, as you switch to another command tab or command group. For example, N can be the Insert tab, or New window in View.

FD

G

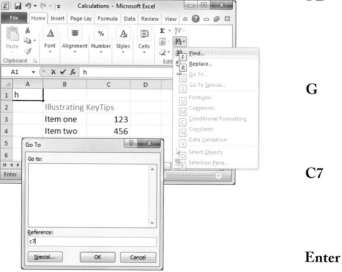

C7

Enter

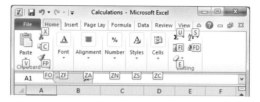

2 The active cell changes to C7, the cell address specified

To select AutoSum, press these keys:

Alt

H

U

S

Enter

Don't forget

For tasks that you
perform often, the
KeyTips option can
become the quickest
way to operate, as you
become familiar with the
keystrokes needed.

Minimize the Ribbon

1 Right-click the Tab bar, or the Quick Access bar, and select Minimize the Ribbon, or double-click any of the command tabs on the Ribbon, or press keys Ctrl+F1

Don't forget

To redisplay the Ribbon fully, repeat any of these actions. You can also minimize the ribbon with the button at the side of the Tab bar. Click it again to expand the ribbon.

2 With the Ribbon minimized, single-click a tab to display the Ribbon temporarily, to select commands from that tab

Hot tip

When you close down Excel with the Ribbon minimized, it will still be minimized when Excel restarts. When the Ribbon is fully displayed at close down, it will be displayed on restart.

3 The Alt key and the KeyTips still operate, even when you have the Ribbon minimized

Quick Access Toolbar

The Quick Access Toolbar contains a set of commands that are independent of the particular Command tab being displayed. There are initially three commands (Save, Undo, and Redo) plus a Customize button, but you can add other commands. By default, the Quick Access Toolbar is located above the File tab, but you can move it below the Ribbon.

1 Right-click the Command tab bar, and select Show Quick Access Toolbar Below the Ribbon

2 To restore the default, right-click the Command tab bar, then select Show Quick Access Toolbar Above the Ribbon

3 To add a command, click Customize Quick Access Toolbar

4 Choose a command from the list, or select More Commands

5 Choose a command category; select a command; click Add, and then click OK

Hot tip

The instruction on the menu is modified to show the reverse process.

Don't forget

You can also right-click any command on the Ribbon, then select Add to Quick Access Toolbar, from the menu.

Mini Toolbar

The Mini toolbar appears when you select text, or when editing the contents of a cell (and also when working with charts and text boxes). It offers quick access to the tools you need for text editing, such as font, size, style, alignment, color, and bullets. To see the mini toolbar:

1 Choose a cell with text content, enter edit mode, by pressing F2, and then select (highlight) part of the text

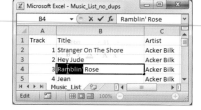

2 The Mini toolbar appears very faintly, being almost completely transparent

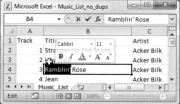

3 Move the mouse pointer towards the Mini toolbar, and the image strengthens

Don't forget

This is a rather transient feature in Excel, but it may be more evident in the mainly text-oriented Word and PowerPoint applications.

4 When the mouse pointer moves over the toolbar, the image solidifies and the toolbar is activated

5 Move the mouse pointer away from the toolbar, and the image fades out and may disappear

This feature was created as an extension of the context (right-click) menu, and it may appear whenever that menu appears.

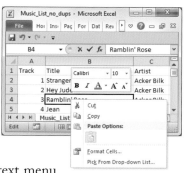

6 Select a cell containing text, press F2, and right-click the cell to see the Mini toolbar above the context menu

Print Worksheets

To preview printing for multiple worksheets:

1 Open the workbook, and click the tab for the first sheet

2 To select adjacent sheets, hold down the Shift key, and click the tab for the last sheet in the group

3 To add other, non-adjacent sheets, hold down the Ctrl key and click the tabs for all of the other sheets required

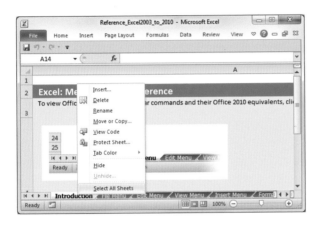

Beware

If you change any cell while multiple sheets are selected, the change is automatically applied to all selected sheets.

4 To select all the sheets, right-click any tab, then click Select All Sheets

5 Click the File tab, and select Print, for the Print Preview and the settings

Alternatively, press the keyboard shortcut Ctrl+F2

If you prefer to use KeyTips shortcuts, press Alt F P V

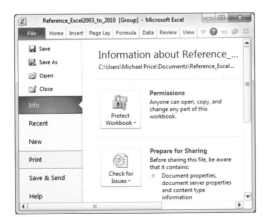

Don't forget

When multiple sheets are selected, the term [Group] appears on the Title bar.

To cancel the selection, click any unselected tab, or right-click any tab and click Ungroup Sheets.

...cont'd

The Preview windows shows print previews for the selected sheets.

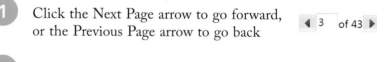

Hot tip

Click the Page Setup link to make detailed changes to the print settings. Click the Printer Properties link to control the printer.

1. Click the Next Page arrow to go forward, or the Previous Page arrow to go back   ◀ 3 of 43 ▶

2. Click the Show Margins button, to display margins, and click and drag the margins to adjust their positions

3. Click the Zoom to Page button to switch between close-up and full page views

4. Click the Settings buttons to adjust items, such as paper size, orientation, scaling, and collation   Portrait Orientation ▼

Don't forget

If the settings are already correct, you can use the Quick Print button (see page 33) to start the Print, without previewing.

5. Click Printer button to select a printer other than the default   Samsung CLP-500 Series   Ready

6. Click the Print button to start the printing
Print

8 Charts

Excel makes it easy to turn your worksheet data into a chart. You can apply formatting, change the type, reselect the data, and add effects, such as 3-D display. Special chart types allow you to display data for stocks and shares. You can print the completed charts on their own, or as part of the worksheet.

Create a Chart

The following information about share purchases and prices will be used for the purpose of illustrating the Excel charting features.

1 Total value of shares in the portfolio at the start of each year (to be charted)

2 The individual prices of the shares on those dates (for calculations)

Portfolio Valuation / Share Prices

Date	AAPL	DELL	IBM	MSFT	RYCEY	WMT	Total	AAPL	DELL	IBM	MSFT	RYCEY	WMT
1/1/1997	99.18	99.60	99.42	91.96	95.82	98.40	584.38	5.22	3.32	33.14	8.36	15.97	9.84
1/1/1998	62.32	315.00	138.18	143.99	83.40	171.90	914.79	3.28	10.50	46.06	13.09	13.90	17.19
1/1/1999	194.37	1098.00	245.22	308.88	92.58	356.80	2295.85	10.23	36.60	81.74	28.08	15.43	35.68
1/1/2000	488.30	1530.00	288.30	520.08	78.60	608.20	3513.48	25.70	51.00	96.10	47.28	13.10	60.82
1/1/2001	141.36	523.20	228.24	193.27	62.40	469.70	1618.17	7.44	17.44	76.08	17.57	10.40	46.97
1/1/2002	208.05	815.40	326.40	295.13	52.20	511.70	2208.88	10.95	27.18	108.80	26.83	8.70	51.17
1/1/2003	136.04	802.20	210.66	230.34	38.88	451.50	1869.62	7.16	26.74	70.22	20.94	6.48	45.15
1/1/2004	203.11	1019.40	253.83	245.96	78.48	477.40	2278.18	10.69	33.98	84.61	22.36	13.08	47.74
1/1/2005	611.80	1264.20	272.10	268.40	123.72	479.80	3020.02	32.20	42.14	90.70	24.40	20.62	47.98
1/1/2006	1365.91	898.50	229.02	265.98	196.44	430.40	3386.25	71.89	29.95	76.34	24.18	32.74	43.04
1/1/2007	1611.96	752.70	274.29	308.11	238.62	430.90	3616.58	84.84	25.09	91.43	28.01	39.77	43.09
1/1/2008	3763.52	735.30	309.51	372.24	300.60	452.00	5933.17	198.08	24.51	103.17	33.84	50.10	45.20
1/1/2009	1621.65	307.20	245.19	207.02	140.46	542.40	3063.92	85.35	10.24	81.73	18.82	23.41	54.24
1/1/2010	4003.87	430.80	388.95	332.20	230.58	528.40	5914.80	210.73	14.36	129.65	30.20	38.43	52.84

Share Quantities: 19, 30, 3, 11, 6, 10

3 The total number of shares held (constants, for simplicity)

Select the Data

Some chart types, such as pie and bubble charts, require a specific data arrangement. For most chart types, however, including line, column, and bar charts, you can use the data as arranged in the rows or columns of the worksheet.

1 Select the cells that contain the data that you want to use for the chart (or click a cell and let Excel select the data)

Portfolio Valuation

Date	AAPL	DELL	IBM	MSFT	RYCEY	WMT	Total
1/1/1997	99.18	99.60	99.42	91.96	95.82	98.40	584.38
1/1/1998	62.32	315.00	138.18	143.99	83.40	171.90	914.79
1/1/1999	194.37	1098.00	245.22	308.88	92.58	356.80	2295.85
1/1/2000	488.30	1530.00	288.30	520.08	78.60	608.20	3513.48
1/1/2001	141.36	523.20	228.24	193.27	62.40	469.70	1618.17
1/1/2002	208.05	815.40	326.40	295.13	52.20	511.70	2208.88
1/1/2003	136.04	802.20	210.66	230.34	38.88	451.50	1869.62
1/1/2004	203.11	1019.40	253.83	245.96	78.48	477.40	2278.18
1/1/2005	611.80	1264.20	272.10	268.40	123.72	479.80	3020.02
1/1/2006	1365.91	898.50	229.02	265.98	196.44	430.40	3386.25
1/1/2007	1611.96	752.70	274.29	308.11	238.62	430.90	3616.58
1/1/2008	3763.52	735.30	309.51	372.24	300.60	452.00	5933.17
1/1/2009	1621.65	307.20	245.19	207.02	140.46	542.40	3063.92
1/1/2010	4003.87	430.80	388.95	332.20	230.58	528.40	5914.80

2 Click the Insert tab, and then select a chart type (Column for example) from the Charts group

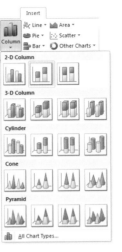

3 Choose the chart subtype, e.g. 2-D Stacked Column (to show how each share contributes to the total value)

4 The chart is superimposed over the data on the worksheet, and Chart Tools (Design, Layout, and Format tabs) are added to the Ribbon

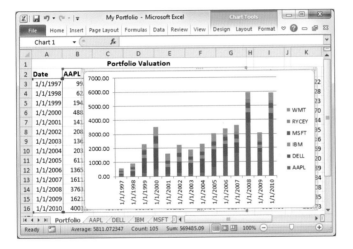

5 Click Move Chart, in the Location group on the Design tab, to choose where you want the chart to be placed, on a separate chart sheet for example

Default Chart Type

You can set any chart type as the default:

1 Click the arrow next to the Charts group name (or click any chart button and select All Chart Types)

The usual default chart type is a 2-D Clustered Column, which compares values across categories, using vertical rectangles.

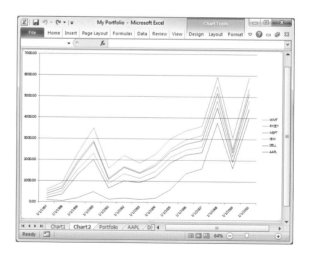

2 On the Insert Chart dialog, choose the chart type and subtype, then click Set as Default Chart, and then click OK

To create a chart based on the default chart type, select the data that you want to use, then press either ALT+F1 or F11.

1 When you press ALT+F1, the chart is embedded in the current worksheet (as shown on page 125)

The 2-D Stacked Line chart shows the trend in the contribution, from each of the categories.

2 When you press F11, the chart is displayed on a separate chart sheet, using the next free name (Chart2 in this case)

Change Chart Layout

1 Click the Chart Tools Layout tab, to modify the chart

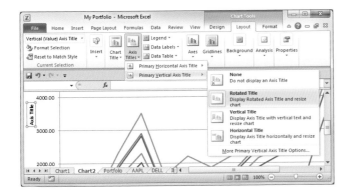

2 Click Axis Titles in the Labels group, and select Primary Vertical Axis Title, then choose the position style

3 Right-click the sample words Axis Title, and select Edit Text, to amend the wording

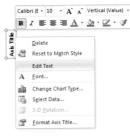

4 Right-click any text and use the Mini toolbar to adjust font styles

Don't forget

Add the Horizontal Axis Title, and the Chart Title similarly, and amend their wording.

127

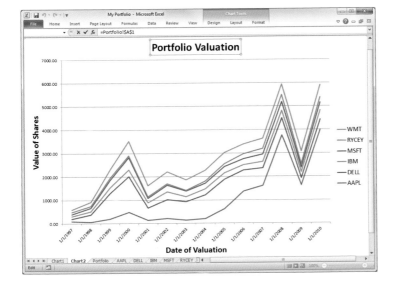

Hot tip

Instead of typing the titles directly, link to a cell on the worksheet. Click in the title, type = on the Formula bar, select the cell with the text, and then press Enter.

Legend and Data Table

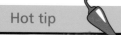

Hot tip

The Legend provides the key to the entries on the chart. In this case, the stock symbols for all of the shares.

1 From the Layout tab, click Labels, Legend, and choose the position and alignment on the chart

Hot tip

You can also display data labels, to show the data values at each point on the lines.

2 Click None to turn off the Legend

3 Click Data Table, in the Labels group, and choose where to position the table, and whether to display the key

Don't forget

You can display the data for the chart in a table, and can include legend keys as well (in which case, the legend itself can be turned off).

Change Chart Type

1 Click the chart area, to display Chart Tools

2 Select the Design tab, and click Change Chart Type from the Type group

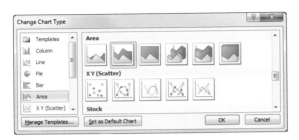

129

Hot tip

As with the Insert Chart dialog, you can make your chosen chart type and subtype the default.

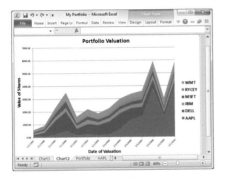

3 In the Change Chart Type dialog, select the chart type and subtype (for example, chart type Area and subtype Stacked Area), then click OK

4 Another way to compare the relative contributions of the shares is to use type Area and subtype 100% Stacked Area

5 A new chart style has been selected from the Shape Styles group, on the Format tab

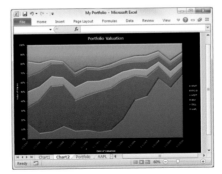

Beware

When you change the chart style, you may need to reapply other changes, such as text font sizes.

Pie Chart

Hot tip

The usual way to compare contributions of individual items to the total is with the Pie Chart. This is intended for a single set of data, one year's share values for example.

Don't forget

The layouts provide several ways to handle the data labels, legend, and data table.

1 Select the data labels and one set of data, in an adjacent row (or hold down Ctrl to select non-adjacent cells)

2 Click the Insert tab, select Pie from the Charts group, and choose the chart type, the standard 2-D Pie Chart for example

3 Click the Design tab, and select Move Chart, to create a chart sheet, Chart3 for example

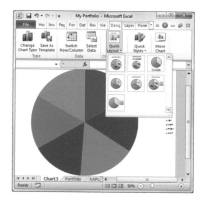

4 Select Quick Layout, in the Chart Layouts group, and choose one of the predefined layouts

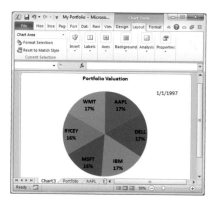

5 This layout shows the data labels, and the relative percentage contributions to the total value, shown on the pie chart segments, rather than using a separate legend box

You can change the data series selected for the pie chart.

1 Select the Chart Tools Design tab, and then click Select Data, in the Data group

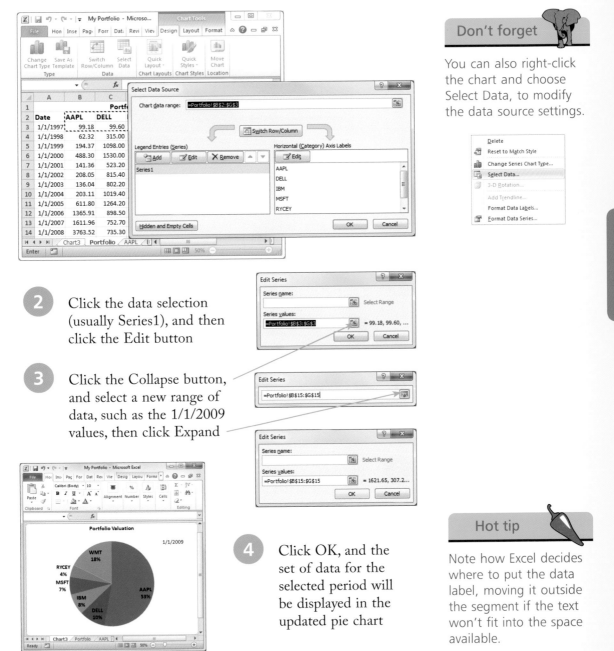

131

Don't forget

You can also right-click the chart and choose Select Data, to modify the data source settings.

2 Click the data selection (usually Series1), and then click the Edit button

3 Click the Collapse button, and select a new range of data, such as the 1/1/2009 values, then click Expand

4 Click OK, and the set of data for the selected period will be displayed in the updated pie chart

Hot tip

Note how Excel decides where to put the data label, moving it outside the segment if the text won't fit into the space available.

3-D Pie Chart

Some of the subtypes for the pie chart offer a 3-D view.

1 Select the Chart Tools Design tab, click Change Chart Type, select Pie, Exploded Pie in 3-D, and then click OK

Don't forget

In a 3-D pie chart, it is the chart segments that are displayed in 3-D format, rather than the data itself (hence the grayed Z component).

2 Select Layout, Background, 3-D Rotation, set rotation values (e.g. X: 0°, Y: 30°, Perspective: 15°), and then click Close

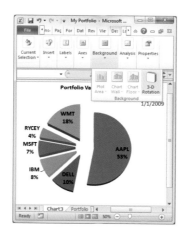

Hot tip

Experiment with the rotation and format options, to find the most effective presentation form for your data.

3 The information is presented in 3-D display form. You can select Chart Tools Format to adjust the appearance, if you wish to add a background color for example

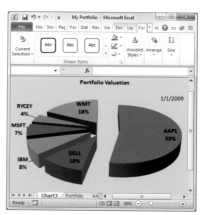

3-D Column Chart

A true 3-D chart has three sets of values to plot, giving three axes. In the example data, these would be Shares, Values, and Dates.

 1 Select the data, click Insert, Charts, Column, and select the 3-D Column chart type

Hot tip

The 3-D Area chart also presents data using three axes, to give a true 3-D representation.

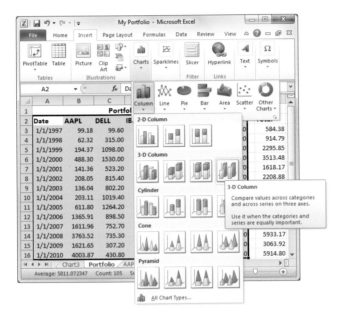

2 Select Chart Tools Design, Layout and Format, to make the desired adjustments to the appearance

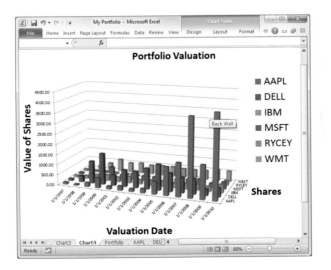

Don't forget

Click Chart Tools, Design, Select Data, and click the Switch Row/Column button to exchange the horizontal and depth axes, to give a different view of the data.

Share Data

The share prices in the portfolio worksheet were taken from price history tables downloaded from the Yahoo Finance website.

 1 Go to finance.yahoo.com, search for the stock code, msft for example, then click the Historical Prices link

Don't forget

The price history table at Yahoo Finance provides information in reverse date sequence, on a daily, weekly, or monthly basis. Use the Adjusted Close values to ensure that the prices are comparable over time.

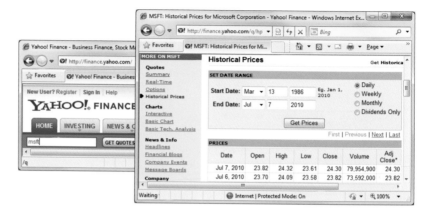

2 Scroll down to the end of the list, and click Download to Spreadsheet

This provides a comma-separated file of dates, prices, and volumes for the selected share. The data can be sorted and converted into an Excel lookup table.

Hot tip

See page 72 for details on converting a range into an Excel table. See page 90 for an example of using the VLOOKUP function.

The table is used to find the price of the share on a given day.

Line Chart

The charts, so far, have used just a few dates from the tables. The complete tables, however, provide a continuous view of the data.

 1 The Historical worksheet contains the date column and adjusted closing price column for each of the shares

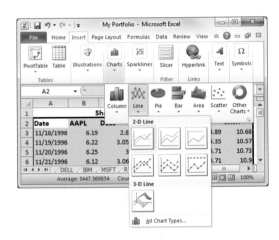

Hot tip

You can choose line, stacked line, or 100% stacked line (with or without markers). There's also a 3-D line, but this is just a perspective view, not three axes of data.

 2 Select the data, click Insert, Chart and Line, then choose the 2-D Line chart subtype, to get a plot for each share

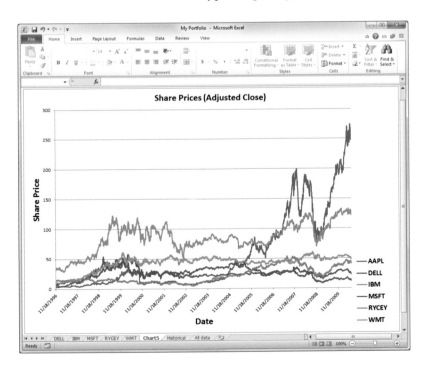

Don't forget

As with all the charts, you can move this chart to a separate chart sheet and adjust position and styles for the titles and the legend.

Stock Chart

The downloaded share data can also be used for a special type of chart, known as the Stock Chart.

 1 From the share table, filter the data (e.g. for 2002), and then select the columns for Date, High, Low, and Close

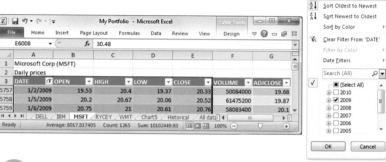

2 Open the Insert Chart dialog (see page 126), select the Stock charts, select type Open-High-Low-Close, and then click OK

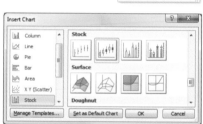

3 The prices are plotted, with lines for high/low, hollow boxes for increases, and solid boxes for decreases

Mixed Types

You can have more than one type of chart displayed at the same time, as in the Volume subtypes of the stock chart.

 Insert a worksheet column after the Date column, and move the Volume column to that position

137

Hot tip

You need to rearrange the data downloaded from Yahoo Finance, to create the volume stock charts, since volumes must be listed before prices.

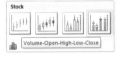

2 Select the data, including the headings, and Insert the Stock chart, choosing type Volume-Open-High-Low-Close

3 Two vertical axes are used, to show volumes and prices

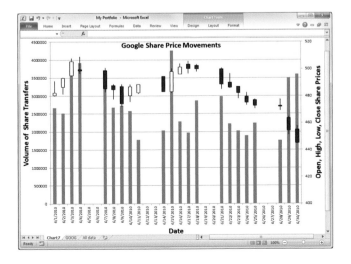

Don't forget

In this example, the two types of chart use the same horizontal values (dates). When necessary, however, Excel will specify a secondary horizontal axis.

Print Charts

When you have an embedded chart in your worksheet, it will be printed, as positioned, along with the data, when you select Print from the File tab, and click the Print button.

To print the chart on its own:

 Select the chart, then select Print from the File tab

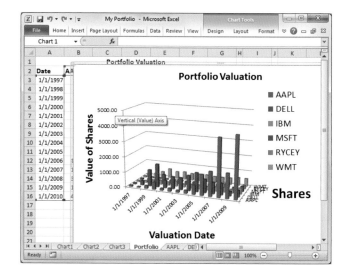

 An extra "Print what" option (Selected Chart) appears, and the other options are grayed, so only the chart will print

9 Macros in Excel

If there are tasks that you carry out frequently, you can define the actions required, as a macro. You can assign the macro to a key combination, or to an icon on the toolbar, to make it easy to reuse. However, you must make sure that security is in place to prevent abuse.

Macros

Any task in Excel may be performed by a macro. Macros are often used to carry out simple but repetitive tasks, such as entering your name and address, or inserting a standard piece of text. In other cases, macros may be used for complex and involved tasks, difficult to reproduce accurately without some kind of help.

To create a macro, you simply carry out an example of the actions, with Excel recording the keystrokes involved as you complete the task. The sequence is then stored as a macro, using the Visual Basic for Applications programming language. You can edit your recorded macros, or create macros from scratch, using the Visual Basic Editor.

Macros can be very powerful, because they are able to run commands on your computer. For this reason, Microsoft Excel prevents the default Excel 2010 file format (file type .xlsx) from storing VBA macro code.

Don't forget

To check which type of workbook you have open, tell Windows to reveal the file type (see page 37).

Therefore, the recommended place for storing the macros you create is in your hidden Personal Macro Workbook, and this is the method used for the examples in the following pages.

If you share macros, they need to be stored in the workbooks that use them. These workbooks must then be saved in the Excel 2010 macro-enabled file format (file type .xlsm). In such cases, you may need to reset the security level, temporarily, to enable all macros, so that you can work on macros in the active workbook:

1 Select File tab, Options, Trust Center, then click the Trust Center Settings and select Macro Settings

Beware

Enable all macros is not recommended as a permanent setting. Select a more restricted level as soon as you have finished creating or changing the macros stored in your active workbook.

2 Select the setting to enable all macros

Create Macros

To display the commands for recording and viewing macros:

1 Select the View tab, and click the arrow below the Macros button, in the Macros group

2 You can choose to view or record macros, and there's also a toggle to choose between relative or absolute cell references

These options are also available from the Developer tab, along with the Macro Security and Visual Basic commands. By default, this tab is not displayed. To add the Developer tab to the Ribbon:

1 Click the File tab, and then select Options (or press the keys Alt F T) and choose Customize Ribbon

2 Click the Developer box, in the Main Tabs section, and the Developer tab will be added to the tab bar

Don't forget

Selecting the Macros button, rather than the arrow, has the same effect as selecting the View Macros entry.

Hot tip

You can record, view, and edit macros, using commands from either the View tab or the Developer tab, but to create macros from scratch, or to change security settings, you will need to use the Developer tab.

Record a Macro

Assume that you need to add some standard disclaimer text to a number of workbooks. To create a macro for this:

1 Open a blank workbook, and click in cell A1

2 Select the Developer tab, then, from the Code group, click Use Relative References, and click Record Macro

3 Enter a name for the macro, and specify a shortcut key, such as Shift+D (the Ctrl key is automatically added)

4 Select Personal Macro Workbook (the preferred location for storing macros), add a description, if desired, and then click OK, to start the recording

5 Perform the actions that you want to record, then select the Developer tab, Code group, and click Stop Recording

To check out the macro:

6 Click in a different cell, C5 for example, and press Shift+Ctrl+D to try out the macro

Don't forget

If there are problems with the macro, you may be able to use the Visual Basic Editor to make the changes that are needed (see page 148).

7 The text is entered into the worksheet, in the active cell

The start location changes, because the macro was created with relative references. However, if you click in any specific cells while the macro is being recorded, those references will be honored.

When you have finished checking the macro, close the workbook:

1 Click the File tab, and select Close

2 Select No, when asked if you want to save changes

Beware

The relative reference applies to the macro, as the initial cell was selected before macro recording was started.

The macro, itself, will be retained in the Personal Macro Workbook. This will be saved at the end of the Excel session (see page 144).

Active Workbooks Macros

If you selected to store the recorded macro in the active workbook, you must save that workbook as file type .xlsm. You will also need to reset the level of macro security (see page 140).

When you close the active workbook, the macros it contains will no longer be available in that Excel session.

Apply the Macro

Don't forget

The macro remains available throughout the Excel session, if you stored it in the Personal Macro Workbook, and you can apply it to any Excel workbook (.xlsm, .xlsx, or .xls types). Once saved, it will be available in future sessions.

1 Open a workbook that requires the disclaimer text, and select the location (e.g. My Personal Budget, cell A16)

2 Press the shortcut key, Shift+Ctrl+D, to run the macro

3 Save the worksheet (no need to change the file type)

Hot tip

The workbook type does not need to be changed to .xlsm, since you are adding text to it, not the actual macro code.

Don't forget

If you choose not to save in the Personal Macro Workbook, any macros created during this Excel session will be lost. This can be a useful way of trying out new ideas, without commitment.

4 When you end the Excel session, you can save your Personal Macro Workbook, and, with it, any macros that you have created during the session

View the Macro

1 Select the View tab, then, from the Window group, click Unhide

2 Select Personal.xlsb, which is your Personal Macro Workbook, and then click OK

145

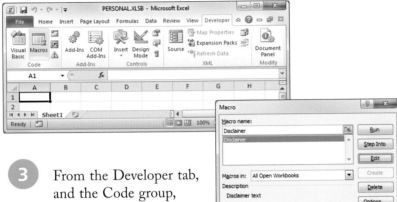

3 From the Developer tab, and the Code group, select Macros

4 Select the macro, and click Edit, to display the code in the VB Editor

5 Select File, Save Personal.xlsb, to save any changes. To finish, select File, Close and Return to Microsoft Excel

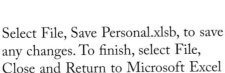

Don't forget

You can view and edit the macro. However, since it is stored in a hidden workbook, you must start by making the workbook visible.

Hot tip

You can make changes to the macro, e.g. revise the text that is entered into the cells, even if you don't know the VBA language.

Beware

When you've finished viewing or changing your macros, select View, Hide, to hide the Personal Macro Workbook.

Macro to Make a Table

1 Open a share history file, YHOO.csv for example

2 Select Developer, Use Relative References, and then click Record Macro

3 Specify the macro name, shortcut, and description, then click OK, to start recording

The steps in the process are as follows:

1 Go to cell A3 (the start of the data range)

Alt H FD G A3 Enter

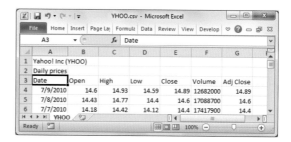

2 Select the whole data range (A3:G3358 in this example) using the End and Arrows keys

ShiftDown End RightArrow End DownArrow ShiftUp

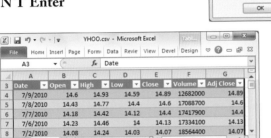

Don't forget

This shows the data range selected, ready for creating the Excel table.

 3 Create an Excel Table from the data

Alt N T Enter

Don't forget

The table is created, but the date column is in descending order (unsuitable for a lookup table).

4 Go to cell A4 (the date field in first row of actual data)

Alt H FD G A4 Enter

5 Sort the column in ascending date sequence

Alt A SA

Beware

If you create an Excel table in a .csv file, you must Save As Excel Workbook (.xlsx format), to retain the table (see page 149).

6 Click Developer, Stop Recording, to complete the macro

147

Edit the Macro

Hot tip

Check the recorded macro, to see if any changes are needed.

1 Unhide the Personal Macro Workbook (see page 145)

2 Select Developer, and then Macros, from the Code group

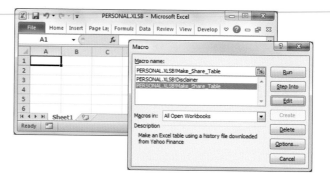

Don't forget

Sections of the macro may be specific to the original workbook. In this case, there are references to the worksheet name. These can be replaced by the generic reference to ActiveSheet.

3 Select the Make_Share_Table macro, and click Edit, to display the code in the Visual Basic Editor

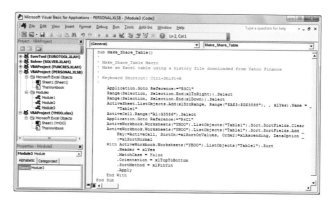

4 Select Edit, Replace, to replace Worksheets("YHOO") by ActiveSheet, and then click the Replace All button

Beware

You should hide the Personal Macro Workbook when you have finished making changes to the macro.

5 Select File, Save and Return to Microsoft Excel (or press Alt+Q)

Use the Macro

1 Open another share history file (ibm.csv for example) that needs to be changed to an Excel table

2 Press the macro shortcut key, Shift+Ctrl+M, and the data range is immediately converted to Excel table format

3 Save the worksheet as file type Excel Workbook (.xlsx)

Repeat this for any other share history files, which can each be converted to Excel table format with a single click of the Make_Share_Table macro shortcut key.

Follow a similar procedure to create and test macros for any other tasks that you need to complete on a regular basis.

Beware

As written, the macro assumes that the worksheet will have data in rows 6 to 533 (ten years). If there are fewer actual rows, the remainder will appear as empty table rows.

Hot tip

Since the macro now refers to the ActiveSheet, it converts the data range in the current worksheet, without regard to its name.

Don't forget

The macro remains in the Personal Macro Workbook, so the share workbooks do not need to be macro-enabled.

Create Macros with VBA

Hot tip

The Music List from Chapter 3 is used here, to illustrate the use of Visual Basic to create a macro, in this case, to insert page breaks after each album.

Hot tip

You'll find sample code for macros such as this on the Internet, at msn.microsoft.com for example.

Don't forget

This macro identifies the last non-blank row in the worksheet. It checks the values in column 4 (Album name), and inserts a page break whenever the name changes.

1 Display the Developer tab on the Ribbon (see page 141)

2 Select the Developer tab, and then, from the Code group, select Visual Basic

3 Click the VBAProject for Personal.xlsb, and then select Insert, Module

4 In the code window for the module, type (or paste) the code for your macro

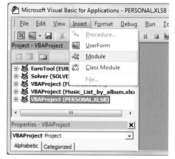

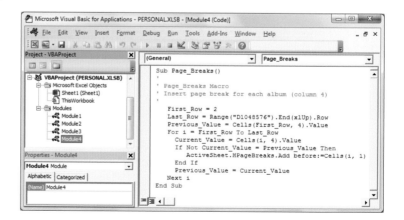

5 When you have entered and checked the macro code, select File, Save and Return to Microsoft Excel

6 In the Music_list worksheet, click the Page Break Preview button on the status bar, to see the page setup

To apply page breaks based on albums:

1 Select the Developer tab, and click the Macros button

2 Select the Page_Breaks macro, and then click Run

3 Manual page breaks are inserted at every change of album in the worksheet data range

151

4 Select Page Layout, Print Titles, to replicate the headings on every page

Add Macros to the Toolbar

If you specified a Ctrl or Shift+Ctrl shortcut when you created your macro, you can run the macro by pressing the appropriate key combination. You can also run the macro by clicking the Macros button, from the View tab or the Developer tab. To make macros more accessible, you can add the View Macros option to the Quick Access Toolbar.

Don't forget

You could also right-click the Macros button, and select Add to Quick Access Toolbar.

1 Select File, Options, and select Quick Access Toolbar, then Choose commands from Popular Commands

2 Click View Macros, click Add, and click OK, View Macros appears on the Quick Access Toolbar

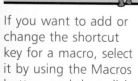

Don't forget

If you want to add or change the shortcut key for a macro, select it by using the Macros button, and then click the Options button.

3 To run a macro, click the View Macros button on the toolbar, select the macro, and click Run

Alternatively, you can add macros as individual icons on the Quick Access Toolbar.

 1 Open Excel Options, select Quick Access Toolbar, and Choose commands, from Macros

2 Scroll down to the particular macros, select each one in turn, and click Add

3 Each macro will have the same icon. You can click Modify, and select a different icon

4 The icons for the macros are added to the Quick Access toolbar

153

Hot tip

Macros can also be associated with graphics, or hot spots on the worksheet.

5 The tooltip shows the name of the macro, which runs immediately when you select its icon

Debug Macros

If you are having a problem with a macro, or if you are just curious to see how it works, you can run it one step at a time.

1 Select Macros, from Developer (or from View), choose the macro you want to run, and click Step Into

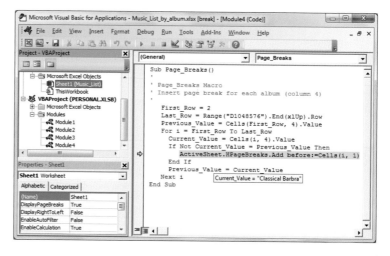

2 Press F8 repeatedly to run through the code, one step at a time

Don't forget

Open a worksheet for which the macro was written, before selecting the Step In option.

3 Hold the mouse over a variable, to see its current value

4 Select Debug, to see the other testing options available, such as setting breakpoints

Hot tip

The breakpoint is the macro statement at which execution will automatically stop. The breakpoints you set will not be saved with the code when you exit.

5 Press F5 to continue to the next breakpoint (or to complete the macro, if no breakpoints are set)

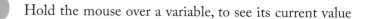

10 Templates and Scenarios

For the most frequent uses of Excel, you'll usually find ready-made templates to give you a head start. There are other Excel resources at the Microsoft Office website. Excel also has special problem-solving tools.

Templates

You can save effort, and you may discover new aspects of Excel, if you base your new workbooks on available templates.

1 Click the File tab, and then click New (or press Ctrl+N), to see the blank workbook and other available templates

2 Click Sample Templates, and select any template to see a preview in the pane on the right

3 Select the template you want to use, the Loan Amortization template for example, and click Create

4 Enter data in the input boxes, so that you can check out the way the workbook operates

Hot tip

Enter data, and then make changes to the values, to see the effect. For example, specify 12 payments per annum, and then change to 2 payments.

5 The worksheet is extended by the number of payments, and displays the calculated amounts

6 To view the formulas behind the calculations, press Ctrl+` (or select the Formulas tab and click Show Formulas)

Beware

You'll find the worksheet is designed for periods of up to 40 years.

157

7 Select the Formulas tab and click the Name Manager button (or press Ctrl+F3), to see the names defined in the workbook, with values and references

Don't forget

To keep the results, you need to save the workbook – the default name is the template name, with a number appended.

Online Templates

To obtain more workbook templates, you can download them from the Microsoft Office Online website.

1 Select File, New, and click a category in the Office Online section, then select a template, to see a preview

2 Click the Download button, to retrieve the selected template from the website

3 A new workbook (based on the downloaded template) will be displayed, ready for updating

The templates that you download will be listed in your personal templates area, for use the next time you create a workbook.

1 Select File, Options, New, and click MyTemplates

2 The templates that you have downloaded are shown

Templates you have used to create workbooks are listed separately.

1 Select File, Options, New, Recent Templates

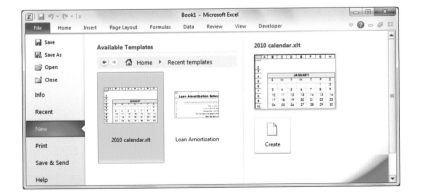

More Excel Resources

The Internet is a prolific source of advice and guidance for Excel users at all levels. Here are some websites that may prove useful:

Don't forget

A search on Google.com, with Excel-related search terms, will result in millions of matches, so it may be easier to start from a more focused website, such as Microsoft Office.

1 Go to office.microsoft.com, and click Support, All support

 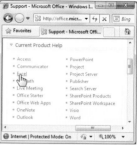

Hot tip

Select All Categories, for the complete list of Excel 2010 Help and How-to articles, videos, and tutorials.

2 Select the Excel link for help getting started, and for a list of related articles and useful links

Beware

The actual links and content for these web pages change continually, but you should expect to find links similar to those shown.

3 Click the Excel MVPs link, to list the Microsoft specialists who deal particularly with Excel, and follow the links to their websites to find topics of interest

4 MVP John Walkenbach's website spreadsheetpage.com, for example, has lots of free tips, downloads, and sample code

If you are interested in creating Excel functions and macros, visit the developer's center.

1 At office.microsoft.com, click More, and select Office for Developers

2 Click Products, and select Excel Developer Center

Hot tip

You'll find that many references relate to Excel 2007 or older versions. These will often be just as applicable when you are running Excel 2010.

3 Explore the contents of the Center, and related sites

What-If Analysis

What-If analysis involves the process of changing values in cells, to see how those changes affect the outcome on the worksheet. A set of values that represent a particular outcome is known as a scenario. To create a scenario:

Don't forget

Sometimes you can set up your worksheet so that several outcomes are visible at once (as in the PMT example on page 93). You can achieve a similar effect by using What-If analysis, and defining scenarios.

1 Open the worksheet, and enter details for a loan, a 25-year mortgage for example

Hot tip

In this case, the scenarios explore the effects of making extra payments, with the first scenario having an extra payment of zero.

2 Select the Data tab, and, from the Data Tools group, click What-If Analysis, Scenario Manager

3 Click Add, type a scenario name (e.g. X000), enter the references for cells that you want to change, and then click OK

4 Change cells from their initial values, as required, in this case, adjusting the value of Scheduled_Extra_Payments

5 Repeat steps 3 & 4 for each scenario, incrementing by 50 (i.e. X050, X100,... X350), and clicking OK for the last one

Hot tip

Additional input cells (Loan_Amount and Loan_Years) have been selected. They have been left unchanged for these scenarios, but give the option for other scenarios in a future analysis.

6 Select a scenario, and click Show, to display any of the results on the worksheet

7 Select Close, to end the Scenario Manager and return to the worksheet

163

Don't forget

You can click Edit to make changes, or corrections, to a scenario, or click Delete to remove unwanted scenarios.

The results from the scenario that was last shown will be displayed. If no scenario was left selected in the Scenario Manager, the original worksheet values will be shown.

Summary Reports

To create a scenario summary report, showing all the possible outcomes on one worksheet:

1 On the Data tab, in the Data Tools group, click What-If Analysis, click Scenario Manager, and then click Summary

2 Choose report type, Scenario summary

It isn't essential to select result cells to generate a scenario summary report, though you would normally want to include values that reflect outcomes.

3 Enter the references for the cells that you want to track (cells with values modified by the changes in scenario values)

4 The outcomes for each of the scenarios are calculated, and the results placed on a new worksheet called Scenario Summary

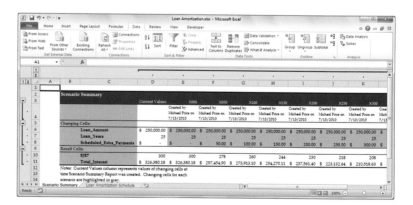

The Changing Cells section displays the values for each scenario of the cells that were selected, when the scenarios were created. The Result Cells section shows the values of the cells specified, when the summary report was created. The Current Values column shows the original values, before the scenarios were defined.

...cont'd

The results can also be presented as a Scenario PivotTable report:

1 Open the Scenario Manager, click Summary, choose Scenario PivotTable report, and enter the references for the result cells

Beware

You must switch back to the Loan Amortization Schedule worksheet, before opening the Scenario Manager.

2 The results are shown in a table on a separate worksheet

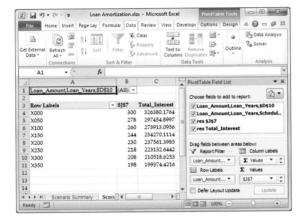

Hot tip

To generate a Scenario PivotTable report, it is always necessary to specify the relevant result cells.

3 Select the PivotTable Tools Options tab, then select PivotChart, from the Tools group, choose the type of chart, Line Chart for example, and then click OK

Don't forget

As with any charts, you can select Design, Move Chart, and place the PivotChart on a separate worksheet.

Goal Seek

If you know the result that you want from an analysis, but not the input values the worksheet needs to get that result, you can use the Goal Seek feature. For example, you can use Goal Seek in the Loan Amortization worksheet, to determine the extra payment required to keep total interest below $150,000.

Hot tip

Start off with the original data scenario, and the extra payment value will be incremented, until the target interest level has been achieved.

1   Select Data, Data Tools, What-If Analysis, and Goal Seek

Scenario Manager...
Goal Seek...
Data Table...

2   For Set cell, enter the reference for the cell with the target value (cell J9).

3   In the box for To value, type the result you want (150000)

Goal Seek

Set cell: J9
To value: 150000
By changing cell: D10

OK   Cancel

Don't forget

The By changing cell must be referred to by the formula in the Set cell, where the changes should be reflected.

4   In the box for By changing cell, enter the reference for the cell that contains the value you want to adjust (D10)

5   The value in D10 is rapidly varied, and the worksheet continually recalculated, until the target value of interest is reached

Goal Seek Status

Goal Seeking with Cell J9 found a solution.

Target value: 150000
Current value: $150,000.00

Step
Pause

OK   Cancel

Beware

The references for the Set cell, and for the By changing cell, must be to single cells only.

6   Click OK to return to the worksheet, with the computed result (and save it as a scenario, if desired)

Optimization

Goal Seek allows you to solve problems where you want to find the value of a single input, to generate the desired result. It is of no help when you need to find the best values for several inputs. For this, you require an optimizer, a software tool that helps you find the best way to allocate resources. These could be raw materials, machine time, people time, money, or anything that is in limited supply. The best or optimal solution will perhaps be the one that maximizes profit, or minimizes cost, or meets some other requirement. All kinds of situations can be tackled in this way, including allocating finance, scheduling production, blending raw materials, routing goods, and loading transportation.

Hot tip

Relationships between the objective, constraints, and decision variables are analyzed to decide the best solution, to satisfy the requirements.

Excel includes an add-in optimizer, called Solver. You may need to install this (see page 103) if it doesn't appear on your system. To illustrate the use of Solver, we'll examine a product mix problem.

Sample Solver Problem

Imagine that your hobby is textiles, and that you produce craft goods (ponchos, scarves, and gloves). There's a craft fair coming up, and you plan to use your existing inventory of materials (warp, weft, and braid) and your available time (for the loom, and to finish goods). You want to know the mix of products that will maximize profits, given the inventory and time available. These include 800 hanks of warp, 600 hanks of weft, 50 lengths of braid, 300 hours of loom time, and 200 hours of finishing time.

To produce a poncho, you will need 8 units of warp, 7 of weft, 1 of braid, 6 for loom, and 2 for finish. For a scarf, the values are 3 warp, 2 weft, 0 braid, 1 loom, and 1 finish. For a pair of gloves, they are 1 warp, 0 weft, 0 braid, 0 loom, and 4 finish.

Don't forget

The problem description must be in sufficient detail, to establish the relationships and identify the constraints.

You make the assumption that your profit is $25 per poncho, $10 per scarf, and $8 per pair of gloves.

You remember that you need four of each item as samples, to show the visitors to the fair. Also, you recall that usually half the scarves are sold in sets with gloves.

Project Worksheet

The craft fair optimization information (see page 167) can be expressed in a worksheet, as follows:

		Resources			Projects				Production		
		Available	Used		Poncho	Scarf	Gloves		Poncho	Scarf	Gloves
Warp		800	310		8	3	1	Net value per item	25	10	8
Weft		600	250		7	2	0				
Braiding		50	30		1	0	0	Quantity created	30	20	10
Loom		300	200		6	1	0				
Finish		200	120		2	1	4	Total income			
									1030		

Wool'n'Weave Project Plan

The worksheet captures the information about resources available, and the amounts needed for any specified level of production.

The formulas that are included in the spreadsheet are:

		Resources		Projects				Production			
		Available	Used	Poncho	Scarf	Gloves			Poncho	Scarf	Gloves
Warp	800	=SUMPRODUCT(F4:H4,$K$6:$M$6)	8	3	1	Net value per item	25	10	8
Weft	600	=SUMPRODUCT(F5:H5,$K$6:$M$6)	7	2	0				
Braiding 50		=SUMPRODUCT(F6:H6,$K$6:$M$6)	1	0	0	Quantity created	30	20	10
Loom	300	=SUMPRODUCT(F7:H7,$K$6:$M$6)	6	1	0				
Finish	200	=SUMPRODUCT(F8:H8,$K$6:$M$6)	2	1	4	Total income			
						=SUMPRODUCT(K4:M4,K6:M6)			

Wool'n'Weave Project Plan

Sample values for the production quantities have been inserted, just to check that the worksheet operates as expected. Excel Solver will be used to compute the optimum quantities.

There are some limitations or constraints that must be taken into account. These are:

1 You cannot exceed the available resources

2 There must be at least 4 of each product (samples for the craft show)

3 There must be whole numbers of products (integers)

4 There must be a pair of gloves each, for at least half the scarves (so that sets can be offered for sale)

Some constraints are specified in the problem description, while others may be implicit (e.g. the requirement for integer (and positive) values of production).

Solver

To calculate the optimum solution for the craft fair problem:

1 Click the cell J9, which contains the target value Total Income, then select the Data tab, and click Solver in the Analysis group

Data
Data Analysis
Solver

Analysis

2 Choose the Max option. Then click the By Changing Cells box, and use the Collapse and Expand buttons to select the product quantities cells (K6:M6)

Hot tip

Solver will use the currently selected cell as the target, unless you replace this reference with another cell.

3 Click the Add button, and select cells to specify that resources used must be less than or equal to those available

4 Click Add, and select cells to specify that quantities produced must be greater than or equal to 4

Don't forget

Click Add, to define the next constraint, or click OK, to return to the Solver Parameters panel.

5 Add the constraint that quantities must be integers

169

...cont'd

6 Specify that the quantity of gloves must be at least half the quantity of scarves, and then click OK

Add Constraint

Cell Reference: $M$6 >= Constraint: =$L$6/2

OK   Add   Cancel

Beware

If you add an Integer constraint, click the Options button, to check that such constraints are currently enabled.

Options

All Methods | GRG Nonlinear | Evolutionary

Constraint Precision: 0.000001

☐ Use Automatic Scaling

☐ Show Iteration Results

Solving with Integer Constraints

☐ Ignore Integer Constraints

Integer Optimality (%):   5

OK   Cancel

Solver Parameters

Set Objective: $J$9

To: ● Max   ○ Min   ○ Value Of: 0

By Changing Variable Cells:

$K$6:$M$6

Subject to the Constraints:

$M$6 >= $L$6/2
$D$4:$D$8 <= $C$4:$C$8
$K$6:$M$6 = integer
$K$6:$M$6 >= 4

Add
Change
Delete
Reset All
Load/Save

☐ Make Unconstrained Variables Non-Negative

Select a Solving Method: GRG Nonlinear

Options

Help   Solve   Close

7 Click Solve, and the results are calculated and displayed

8 If Solver found a solution, click Keep Solver Solution, clear Return to Solver Parameters Dialog, then click OK, to return to the workbook

Solver Results

Solver found a solution. All Constraints and optimality conditions are satisfied.

Reports
Answer

● Keep Solver Solution

○ Restore Original Values

☐ Return to Solver Parameters Dialog   ☐ Outline Reports

OK   Cancel   Save Scenario...

Reports

Creates the type of report that you specify, and places each report on a separate sheet in the workbook

Don't forget

The Answer worksheet added each time you run Solver will show the detailed results, and the constraints applied.

WeavingProjects.xlsx - Microsoft Excel

File | Home | Insert | Page Layout | Formulas | Data | Review | View | Developer

J9   =SUMPRODUCT(K4:M4,K6:M6)

	A	B	C	D	E	F	G	H	I	J	K	L	M	N
1							Wool'n'Weave Project Plan							
2			Resources			Projects					Production			
3			Available	Used		Poncho	Scarf	Gloves			Poncho	Scarf	Gloves	
4		Warp	800	479		8	3	1		Net value per item	25	10	8	
5		Weft	600	380		7	2	0						
6		Braiding	50	44		1	0	0		Quantity created	44	36	19	
7		Loom	300	300		6	1	0						
8		Finish	200	200		2	1	4		Total income				
9										1612				

Answer Report 1 | Sheet1 | Sheet2 | Sheet3

Ready   100%

11 Links and Connections

Excel lets you make external references to other workbooks, or to web pages that contain data needed for your active worksheet. Your worksheet is updated automatically, if the source data changes. You can also share your data as an Office document, or as a PDF.

Link to Workbooks

Hot tip

Workbook links are very useful, when you need to combine information from several workbooks that may be created in different locations, or on different systems.

Sometimes you may want to refer to the data in one workbook from another, separate workbook. You may, for example, want to provide an alternative view of the data in a worksheet, or to merge data from individual workbooks, to create a summary workbook. You can refer to the contents of cells in another workbook by creating external references (also known as links).

References may be to a cell or a range, though it is usually better to refer to a defined name in the other workbook.

To establish defined names in a source workbook:

1 Open a source workbook, North.xlsx for example

Don't forget

This shows the sales by quarter, for one region, with the first two quarters entered. The calculations for margin (profit/sales) for the remaining quarters show zero divide errors, since the associated sales values are zero.

2 Select a range of cells, B4:E4 (the costs) for example

3 Select the Formulas tab, and click Define Name, in the Defined Names group

4 Specify the name (or accept the suggested name, e.g. Costs), and then click OK

5 Repeat the Define Name process for names Sales (B5:E5) and Profit (B6:E6)

6 Select the Formulas tab, and click Name Manager, in the Defined Names group, to see all the name definitions

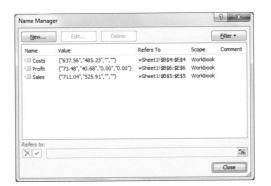

7 Save and close the North workbook

Repeat this for the other source workbooks (in this example, they are South, East, and West), to define range names Costs, Sales, and Profit for each of them.

173

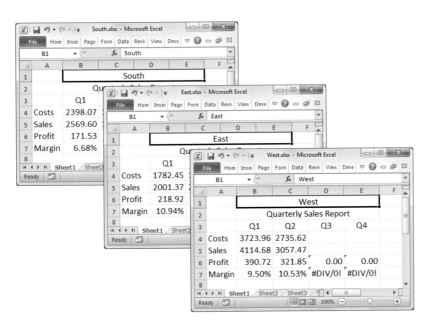

8 Save and close the South, East, and West workbooks

Create External References

1 Open the source workbooks that contain the cells you want to refer to (e.g. North, South, East, and West)

2 Open the workbook that will contain the external references (in the example, it is called Overall.xlsx)

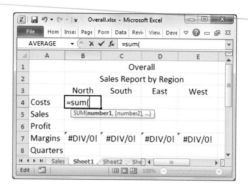

3 Select the cell in which you want to create the first of the external references (e.g. B4) and type (for example) =sum(

4 Select the View tab, and, in the Windows group, click Switch Windows, click the source workbook, and, if necessary, select the worksheet that contains the cells that you want to link to

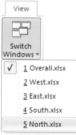

5 Press F3, and select the defined name for the range of cells, e.g. Costs, click OK, and then press Enter

6 Similarly, enter a formula in B5 to sum Sales, and enter a formula in B6 to sum Profit

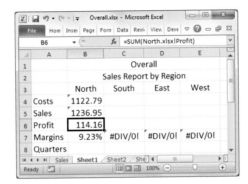

Hot tip

You can copy the formula for Costs, and then change the defined name to Sales or Profit.

You could refer to source workbook cells directly:

1 Click in cell B8, and type =count(

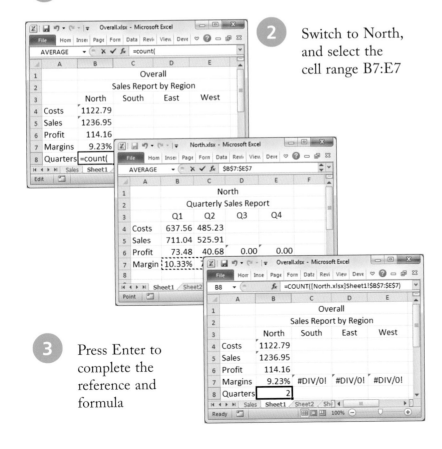

2 Switch to North, and select the cell range B7:E7

3 Press Enter to complete the reference and formula

Don't forget

This function counts the number of cells containing numbers (thus ignoring the incomplete quarters, where the Margin shows Divide by Zero).

Styles of Reference

While the source workbooks are open, the links to defined names take the form:

North.xlsx!Costs

Where you refer to cells directly, the links take the form:

[North.xlsx]Sheet1!$B$7:$E$7

Note that the cell references could be relative or mixed, as well as absolute, as shown.

Close the source workbook, and you'll find that the external references are immediately expanded, to include a fully qualified link to the source workbook file.

176

Hot tip

The references for South, East, and West have been incorporated. You can do this by selection, as with North, or you can just copy the formulas for North, and change the name appropriately.

	A	B	C	D	E	F	G
			Overall				
1			Sales Report by Region				
2		North	South	East	West		
3	Costs	1122.79	4183.39	3673.80	6459.58		
4	Sales	1236.95	4477.43	4115.15	7172.15		
5	Profit	114.16	294.04	441.35	712.57		
6	Margins	9.23%	6.57%	10.73%	9.94%		
7	Quarters	2	2	2	2		

E4 = `=SUM('C:\Users\Michael Price\Documents\West.xlsx'!Costs)`

Links with direct cell references also show the file path and name:

	A	B	C	D	E	F	G	H
1			Overall					
2			Sales Report by Region					
3		North	South	East	West			
4	Costs	1122.79	4183.39	3673.80	6459.58			
5	Sales	1236.95	4477.43	4115.15	7172.15			
6	Profit	114.16	294.04	441.35	712.57			
7	Margins	9.23%	6.57%	10.73%	9.94%			
8	Quarters	2	2	2	2			

E8 = `=COUNT('C:\Users\Michael Price\Documents\[North.xlsx]Sheet1'!$B$7:$E$7)`

In each case, the path and file name will be enclosed in quotation marks, whether there are spaces included or not.

Source Workbook Changes

Assume that you receive new versions of the source workbooks (with the next quarter's data). You can control how these changes affect the destination workbook.

1 Open the destination workbook (leaving the source workbooks closed)

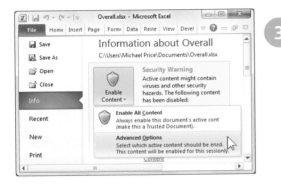

2 The security warning tells you that automatic update is disabled

3 Click the message link to display the BackStage Info, and click Enable Content, then Advanced Options

4 Leave the choice as Help protect me, and click the OK button

5 The workbook opens, without updating the changes

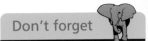

Don't forget

When the source and destination workbooks are open on the same computer, links will be updated automatically.

Hot tip

Click the [X] on the message, to open immediately, without updates. The Enable Content option will make this a Trusted Document, as does choosing Enable All Content, from the Advanced Options.

Apply the Updates

 Select the Data tab, then, in the Connections group, choose Edit Links

Don't forget

You can only update selected entries, if you wish, and you can use the Check Status button to see which entries still need to be applied.

Select the entries you want to refresh, and click the Update Values button

Data changes are applied, and worksheet status is updated

Beware

Do not apply updates where you are unsure of the origin of the changes, or if you want to retain the current values.

Hot tip

To see the trends in Cost, select cell F4, click Insert, pick a Sparklines type, then select the data range (B4:E4). Copy F4 to F5:F7 to display the trends for Sales, Profit, and Margin.

The updated information is added to the destination workbook, which now displays the data for three quarters

Turn Off the Prompt

You can turn off the update prompt for a specific workbook.

1 Open the workbook, select the Data tab, and then click Edit Links, in the Connections group

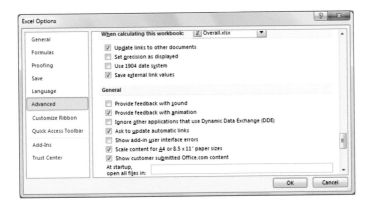

179

Don't forget

If you turn off the alert, and disallow updates, users of the workbook won't know that the data is out of date.

2 Click the Startup Prompt button and choose Don't display the alert, with or without updating, as desired

There is an Excel option to turn off all update prompts. To review this setting:

1 Select the File tab, click Excel Options, and choose the Advanced category

2 There is an option called Ask to update automatic links, which is normally selected

3 Do not clear this option: this would cause automatic updates to be applied to all workbooks, with no prompt

Beware

Do not use this option to turn off the prompt, or you will not be aware when workbooks get updated. Use the workbook-specific method only.

Excel in Word

When you've completed your worksheet, you can present the information in a Microsoft Office Word document (as illustrated here), or in a PowerPoint presentation.

To add data from an Excel worksheet to your Word document:

1 In Excel, select the worksheet data, and press Ctrl+C (or select Home and click Copy, from the Clipboard group)

2 Click in the Word document, and press Ctrl+V (or select Home and click Paste, from the Clipboard group)

Don't forget

You can paste the data as a table, retaining the original formatting, or using styles, from the Word document. Alternatively, paste the data as a picture or tab-separated text. There are also options to maintain a link with the original worksheet.

3 Click Paste Options, and select the type of paste you want

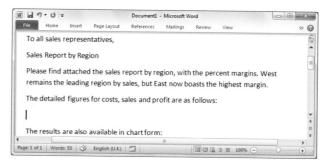

To copy an Excel chart to your Word document:

1 In Excel, select the chart on the worksheet or chart sheet, and press Ctrl+C (or select Home, Clipboard, Copy)

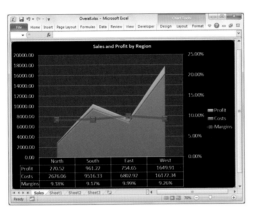

2 In the Word document, click where you want the chart, and press Ctrl+V (or select Home, Clipboard, Paste)

3 Click Paste Options, and select the type you want

Publish as PDF (or XPS)

To send information to others who do not have Excel or Word, you can publish the workbook in the Adobe Acrobat PDF format, which only requires the Adobe Reader, available for no charge from www.adobe.com.

1 Open the workbook in Excel, click the File tab, and then click Save As

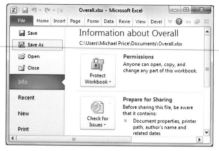

2 Set the Save As type to PDF (or XPS)

3 Click the Options button, to set the scope

4 Select Open file after publishing, and click the Publish button, to create and display the PDF (or XPS) file

Save on the Web

You can store workbooks and other documents online, and access them via Office Web Apps, or share them with other users. To copy a workbook to the SkyDrive from within Excel:

 Open the workbook, click the File tab, and select Save & Send, and then Save to Web

Hot tip

Save workbooks to the Windows Live SkyDrive, to access them from other computers, or to share them with other users.

183

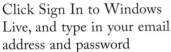 Click Sign In to Windows Live, and type in your email address and password

 Select the SkyDrive folder, and click Save As

Don't forget

You could save in your private documents folder, or in your public folder, but for controlled access, click New, and create a separate SkyDrive folder.

4 Revise the workbook name, if desired, then click Save

Don't forget

Close the workbook from within Excel, when it has been saved, if you want to edit it online via the Excel Web App.

5 Go to office.live.com, and sign in to Windows live

Hot tip

Select documents from your libraries, to copy them as a group to the folder, rather than using Excel to Save & Send them one by one.

6 Select the folder name (in this case Project), and click Add Files, to copy files directly from your computer

Access the SkyDrive Folder

 Select one of the files, and select Edit in Browser

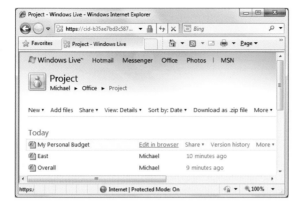

Don't forget

The Excel Web App displays the workbook with a ribbon, but with only the Home tab and a much reduced Insert tab.

 The workbook displays with the Home tab selected

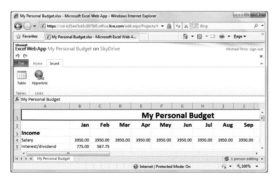

Hot tip

Click the File tab, and you'll see there is no Save function, since any changes will be saved automatically.

3 Click the Insert tab, which has limited functions available

Share Workbooks

1 Open the folder, select the Shared With link, and follow prompts, to specify user names and send notifications

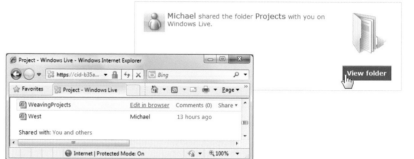

2 Each user receives a message, with a link to the folder

> Michael shared the folder Projects with you on Windows Live.
>
> View folder

3 Click the link, and sign in to Windows Live, you can then choose any file, and select Edit in Browser

4 You can view and change the data, even view (but not create) Excel charts and Sparklines

5 More than one person can edit a workbook at the same time

Index